Good Frien

KEY PORTER BOOKS

Canadian Cataloguing in Publication Data

Main entry under title:

Good friends cookbook

Includes index.
ISBN 1-55013-320-9

1. Cookery. I. Fare for Friends Foundation.

TX714.F66 1991 641.5 C91-093089-9

Key Porter Books Limited
70 The Esplanade
Toronto, Ontario
Canada M5E 1R2

Typesetting: MacTrix DTP

Printed on acid-free paper

Printed and bound in Canada

91 92 93 94 95 6 5 4

A Special Project

Each year, thousands of women across Canada suffer serious physical and psychological abuse. These women must have an avenue of escape and a haven of protection where they can remain safe until they regain their strength.

During the past decade, growing public awareness of the insidious social problem of family violence has provided a stimulus for the creation of halfway houses for abused women and their children in communities across the nation. However, in most cases, it is not possible for such refuges to survive solely dependent on government funding.

For this reason, in 1983, *Fare for Friends* was lovingly compiled and published. Its objective, as a special fund-raising project, was to help sustain Interim Place, one such haven, located in Mississauga, Ontario. Because of the book's great success, the Fare for Friends Foundation has been able to assist Interim Place in specific and meaningful ways. Proceeds from the sale of *Fare for Friends* have provided such vital necessities as salaries for child-care workers and other trained professionals, a creative playground for children, educational opportunities for women in crisis and a much-needed kitchen renovation.

Unfortunately, as is the case with most such hostels, Interim Place too frequently finds itself stretched beyond its capacities. Sadly, when the shelter is full, some women are forced to seek refuge elsewhere. To answer this very real social issue, plans for a second shelter are firmly in place. This facility is designed specifically to meet the requirements of its intended occupants and will create a warm and supportive environment for the positive rebuilding of shattered lives.

Inspired by the realization that a few women with a good project can make a significant difference, the authors of *Fare for Friends* are delighted to present you with a second book.

Again, the cookbook, itself, salutes organizations committed to eliminating family violence everywhere. Your purchase of it will lend valuable support to this cause.

Our book is for you, the cooks who have used, enjoyed and raved about *Fare for Friends*. You've told us, again and again, that the recipes work. Some have said it's the only cookbook they use; another enthused that it was one of the best she had ever owned, and she owns hundreds. Some even claim they couldn't cook until they got this book. You've cajoled, yes, demanded more. Through this outpouring of support and praise, we feel immeasurably enriched by the circle of friendship that has flourished with all of you.

Your enthusiasm has gratified and amazed us. Most of all, it has challenged us to dig in and do it again – to let our enjoyment of good food, creative cooking, and the companionship of friends, lead us back to our kitchens to create recipes using new trends blended with old-fashioned goodness. In short, to produce more wonderful food – for our friends!

Written and compiled by:

Judy Leach, chair	Joyce George
Eleanor Ball	Mary Gilpin
Gail Bascombe	Ruth Kitchen
Lyn Bolt	Wilma Mason
Jane Buckland	Beth Miller
Joan Corbett	Jennifer Porteous
Libby Dal Bianco	Susan Pryce
Jenny Dale	Doreen White

Contents

This book is for Sue Rowland
who loved life.
For her, every day was a Joy,
every meal a Celebration.

Beginnings

Salmon Tortilla Rolls

An elegant unusual hors d'oeuvre – expect raves!

1	package (8 oz/250 g) cream cheese, softened	1	
3	tablespoons mayonnaise	50	mL
3	tablespoons honey mustard	50	mL
6	large flour tortillas	6	
3	tablespoons small capers	50	mL
1	head Boston lettuce	1	
¾	pound pre-sliced smoked salmon	375	g
2	tablespoons snipped fresh dill	25	mL

In a bowl, whip cream cheese, mayonnaise and mustard. Divide and spread on tortillas. Sprinkle with capers and cover with individual lettuce leaves. Place salmon over all. Roll tortillas very tightly and wrap in plastic wrap. Refrigerate for at least 5 to 6 hours. At serving time, cut into ½" (1.5 cm) slices, sprinkle with dill and serve. Skewer with toothpicks if necessary.

Serves 20

* Alternatively, try with cream cheese, horseradish, salami and roasted sweet red pepper.

Seasoned Norwegian Flatbread
Freezer-ready for your convenience!

1	package (8 oz/240 g) Kavli thin Norwegian flatbread	1
1	cup butter, softened	250 mL
2	large cloves garlic, minced	2
⅔	cup grated Parmesan cheese	150 mL
1	tablespoon finely chopped fresh parsley	15 mL

Preheat oven to 325° F (160° C). Place all the flatbread in piles, as it comes out of the package, on a bread board. Using a bread knife, saw the pieces into thirds or halves, cutting several thicknesses at a time. Combine butter, garlic, Parmesan cheese and parsley. Thinly spread the mixture over the flatbread. Place on a cookie sheet and bake for just 5 minutes until lightly browned. Watch closely! Let cool; store in airtight containers. It freezes well. Serve at room temperature.

Serves 20

Our California Pizza

This appetizer or luncheon dish is served cold and best made the day it is to be eaten. The recipe can easily be doubled.

Crust

1	package of refrigerated crescent rolls (8 rolls per package)	1

Filling

1	package (8 oz/250 g) cream cheese, softened	1
⅓	cup mayonnaise	75 mL
2	tablespoons pesto	25 mL
¼	cup slivered sun-dried tomatoes	50 mL
1	small clove garlic, minced	1

Topping

½	sweet red pepper, finely chopped	½
½	sweet green pepper, finely chopped	½
½	bunch broccoli, tops only, finely chopped	½
2	green onions, finely chopped	2
1½	teaspoons vinaigrette	7 mL

Preheat oven to 350° F (180° C). To make crust, lay crescent roll pieces flat on an ungreased cookie sheet. If you want a thinner crust, roll or pat the pieces. Bake for about 11 minutes or until brown. Cool completely.

For the filling, blend cream cheese, mayonnaise and pesto in a food processor or mixer until smooth. Add sun-dried tomatoes and garlic; blend just to combine. Set aside.

In a separate bowl, combine all the topping ingredients. Shortly before serving, spread filling on cooled crust. Sprinkle with topping ingredients, pressing into filling firmly. Refrigerate until ready to serve. Cut into squares.

Serves 8 to 10 as an appetizer, 4 as a luncheon dish

* Try this variation using the same crust.

Filling

1	package (8 oz/250g) cream cheese, softened	1
⅓	cup mayonnaise	75 mL
½	package (1 oz/28 g) Hidden Valley Ranch dressing mix	½
½	cup grated cheese (your choice)	125 mL

Topping

½	cup, each chopped finely, carrots, broccoli tops, cauliflower, sweet green and red pepper	125 mL
¼	cup finely chopped green onions	50 mL
¼	cup seeded and chopped tomatoes	50 mL

Mix the filling ingredients together. Combine all topping ingredients and mix ¾ of them with the filling. Spread over cooled crust. Sprinkle remaining ¼ of vegetables on top to garnish. Chill and serve as above.

Bruschetta with Warm Chèvre Spread

Serve with your favorite wine before a crackling fire on a cold winter night!

2	ripe tomatoes, peeled, seeded and chopped	2
1-2	cloves garlic, minced	1-2
¼-½	cup chopped fresh basil	50-125 mL
	Freshly ground pepper to taste	
6	ounces chèvre	170 g
1-2	tablespoons pine nuts for garnish	15-25 mL
	Toasted French bread or crackers	

Preheat oven to 350° F (180° C). Mix first 4 ingredients together and let stand at room temperature for at least 30 minutes. Place chèvre in a small, round, flat oven-proof dish. Press pine nuts into top. Bake until warm, about 10 minutes. Spoon tomato mixture around chèvre and spread on toasted French bread or crackers.

Serves 6 to 8 as an hors d'oeuvre

Satay Peanut Chicken

The sauce is a big hit.

4	half chicken breasts, boned and skinned	4
½	cup peanut butter	125 mL
½	cup vegetable oil	125 mL
¼	cup white wine vinegar	50 mL
¼	cup soy sauce	50 mL
¼	cup lemon juice	50 mL
4	cloves garlic, minced	4
8	sprigs parsley	8
2	teaspoons crushed dried red pepper	10 mL
2	teaspoons grated fresh ginger	10 mL
8	small bamboo skewers, soaked in water for 30 minutes before threading	8

Warm peanut butter to liquify. In a food processor or by hand, blend all ingredients except chicken. Reserve ¾ cup (175 mL) of the peanut sauce for dipping. Cut chicken into cubes or strips; marinate in sauce for 1 hour at room temperature or overnight in the refrigerator. Remove chicken from marinade; thread onto skewers. Barbecue or broil 10 to 15 minutes, brushing frequently with marinade. Pass the satays with reserved sauce for dipping.

Serves 8

* Satay Peanut Chicken makes a wonderful dinner served with rice and extra sauce for dipping.

* Lean veal, lamb or pork work well, too.

* Instead of bamboo skewers, you can use metal skewers rubbed with oil (rather than soaked with water).

Tuna Truffles

Looks colorful on a canapé tray.

1	can (6 ½ oz/184 g) flaked white tuna, drained	1	
1	package (8 oz/250 g) cream cheese, softened	1	
3	tablespoons sherry	50	mL
1	teaspoon horseradish	5	mL
1¼	cups grated Cheddar cheese	300	mL
½	cup unsweetened flaked coconut	125	mL
¼	teaspoon salt	1	mL
	Pepper to taste		
¼	teaspoon Worcestershire sauce	1	mL
1	bunch parsley, finely chopped	1	
	Red or black caviar for garnish (optional)		

Combine all ingredients, except parsley and caviar, in a food processor or blender; blend until smooth. Chill. (The mixture may be prepared a day in advance or frozen.) Form mixture into tiny balls no bigger than 1" (2.5 cm) in diameter; roll in chopped parsley.

To garnish, in each ball, make a small indentation with baby finger and fill with caviar. Arrange in an attractive pattern on a serving plate by leaving some plain balls and alternating with the truffles filled with red and black caviar.

Feeds a crowd

* Can be served on toothpicks or in truffle cups.

* This is also delicious used as a filling for celery, cherry tomatoes, endive leaves or cucumber rounds.

Keftadas

A light lemony meatball that is good even without a dip.

1	pound lean ground beef	500	g
½	pound feta cheese, finely crumbled	250	g
1	egg, lightly beaten	1	
1	egg white, lightly beaten	1	
2-3	green onions, finely chopped	2-3	
1	clove garlic, minced	1	
¼	cup chopped fresh parsley	50	mL
1	tablespoon chopped fresh oregano or	15	mL
	1 teaspoon (5 mL) dried		
2-2½	tablespoons fresh lemon juice	25-30	mL
	Freshly ground pepper to taste		
	Flour to coat meatballs		
	Vegetable oil for frying		

Place all ingredients except flour and oil in a large bowl. Mix together with a fork. Form into 1" (2.5 cm) balls, squeezing out excess moisture if necessary. Roll meatballs in flour to coat. Heat a little vegetable oil in a frying pan over medium heat. Brown meatballs on all sides until they are cooked through. Remove from pan and drain on paper towel. (To prepare ahead of time, slightly undercook the meatballs and refrigerate. Reheat at serving time in a 350° F (180° C) oven. Meatballs may also be frozen.) Serve with toothpicks as an appetizer.

Makes 48 meatballs

* Yogurt Dip for Keftadas

1	cup low-fat or fat-free yogurt	250	mL
1	tablespoon chopped fresh mint or basil	15	mL
½	teaspoon ground cumin	2	mL
	Freshly ground pepper to taste		

Stir all ingredients together and use as a dip for the meatballs. Store in the refrigerator.

Cambozola Pita Pizzas

Everyone loves this. It's different and very tasty.

4	cooking onions, thinly sliced	4
2	tablespoons butter	25 mL
1-2	tablespoons brown sugar	15-25 mL
4	teaspoons balsamic vinegar or water	20 mL
	Salt and pepper to taste	
1-1½	packages mini pita rounds, halved horizontally	1-1½
8	ounces Cambozola cheese, crumbled	250 g
	Sun-dried tomatoes, slivered	

Preheat oven to 300° F (150° C). Spread onions in a shallow baking dish. Dot with butter; sprinkle with brown sugar, balsamic vinegar, salt and pepper. Bake, covered for 30 to 40 minutes, stirring once. (You may cook these a day or two in advance and store them in the refrigerator.) Near serving time, place pita halves on baking sheets. Top each pita half with a spoonful of onions, Cambozola and 2 to 4 slivers of sun-dried tomatoes. Preheat oven to 375° F (180° C). Just before serving time, bake 6 to 8 minutes until light brown and bubbly.

Makes 50 to 75

Tex-Mex Taco Dip

A new lighter version of an old favorite.

1	package (8 oz/250 mL) cream cheese	1
1	cup cottage cheese	250 mL
1	envelope taco seasoning	1
¾	cup medium or hot salsa (depending on your crowd)	175 mL
½	small head iceberg lettuce, shredded	½
1	tomato, seeded and chopped	1
1	sweet green pepper, chopped	1
1	small onion, chopped	1
½	ripe avocado, chopped (optional)	½
2	cups grated Cheddar cheese (optional)	500 mL
	Taco chips for dipping	

Combine cream cheese, cottage cheese and taco seasoning in a food processor or blender for 30 seconds or until smooth. Refrigerate mixture for several hours before serving. (This can be done a day ahead.) To serve, mound cheese-taco mixture on a large platter. Cover with salsa. Mix prepared vegetables together, including avocado (if using). Cover salsa with about ¾ of the vegetables. Reserve remainder to be added when the hors d'oeuvre begins to look messy. Sprinkle cheese on top (if using). Surround with taco chips.

Serves a crowd

Pesto and Sun-Dried Tomato Torta

Make ahead; enjoy later. Great for the sports crowd or your most elegant guests.

1	package (8 oz/250 g) cream cheese	1	
½	cup butter	125	mL
½	small onion, chopped	½	
¼-½	cup pesto	50-125	mL
½	cup chopped sun-dried tomatoes	125	mL
½	cup toasted pine nuts	125	mL
	Fresh basil leaves or parsley sprigs for garnish		

In a food processor or with a mixer, blend cream cheese and butter until smooth. Stir in onion just to blend. Line a 2-cup (500 mL) bowl with plastic wrap. Layer ⅓ of the cheese mixture in the bottom. Spread with ½ of the pesto, then ½ of the sun-dried tomatoes. (Spread each of these right to the edge so the layers can be seen when unmoulded). Add a second layer of cheese. Spread with remaining pesto, then sun-dried tomatoes. Spread remaining cheese on top. Cover and refrigerate for at least 2 hours or overnight. Unmould at serving time and remove plastic wrap. Press pine nuts into surface. Garnish with fresh basil leaves or parsley sprigs.

Makes about 2 cups (500 mL)

* Serve this spread with crackers or interesting breads.

Roquefort Canapés

Blue-cheese lovers, this is for you!

2	tablespoons grainy Dijon mustard	25	mL
¼	pound Roquefort cheese, crumbled	125	g
¼	cup chopped fresh parsley	50	mL
2	tablespoons mayonnaise	25	mL
24	mushroom caps or	24	
	hollowed-out cherry tomatoes		
	Chopped fresh parsley		
	Pine nuts		

Gently combine mustard, Roquefort, parsley and mayonnaise. Fill mushroom caps or tomatoes. Garnish with parsley and pine nuts.

Makes 24

* This filling is also delicious in Belgian endive leaves or snow peas.

* Some filling left over? Try spreading it on a tomato or chicken sandwich.

The Best of Brie

A creamy indulgence.

	One piece of ripe Brie as large as you need – a wedge to a whole round		
¼-2	cups pecan halves	50-500	mL
¼-2	cups chutney (your favorite variety) or cranberry relish	50-500	mL

An hour or more before serving, remove top rind from Brie carefully with a knife. Allow Brie to come to room temperature. Preheat oven to 300° F (150° C). Toast pecans in oven, on a cookie sheet, for 15 to 20 minutes. Do not allow to burn. Place Brie on an ovenproof platter (or use a cookie sheet and transfer cheese to a platter after baking), spread with enough chutney or relish to cover. Arrange pecans attractively over surface. Bake until cheese begins to melt.

Serves 4 to 25

* Serve with crackers.

* Try Fig Compote (see page 17) as an alternative topping.

Mexican Chili Dip

The whole recipe serves a crowd; halve for just a few friends.

1	cup mayonnaise	250	mL
1	cup sour cream	250	mL
1	package (2.4 oz/77 g) Knorr leek soup mix	1	
2	teaspoons chili powder	10	mL
½	teaspoon ground cumin	2	mL
1	cup shredded Monterey Jack cheese	250	mL
1	cup peeled, seeded and chopped tomato	250	mL
1	can (4 oz/110 mL) green chilies, chopped	1	
2-3	tablespoons chopped jalapeño peppers	25-50	mL
	Chopped fresh chives for garnish		

In a medium bowl, mix together mayonnaise, sour cream, soup mix, chili powder and cumin until smooth. Stir in remaining ingredients except chives; mix well. Cover and refrigerate for at least 2 hours to blend flavors. Present in a pottery bowl; garnish with chopped chives.

Makes 4 cups (1 L)

*This dip can be served with corn chips, tortilla chips or raw vegetables.

Sweet Salami Bites

Spicy salami gives an especially nice contrast to the sauce.

1	large or 2 small beef salamis (1 lb/500 g in total)	1
1	jar (7 ½ oz/213 mL) junior apricots (baby food)	1
¼	cup maple syrup or honey	50 mL
¼	cup Sassy Sauce (see page 193) or sweet Russian mustard with horseradish	50 mL

Preheat oven to 350° F (180° C). Do not use hard, dry salami in this recipe. Cut salami into bite-sized chunks; place in shallow baking dish. Mix remaining ingredients together and pour over salami. Bake for 40 minutes, basting occasionally. Serve with toothpicks.

Serves 12 to 16

* The sauce would be equally good baked with meatballs or chicken wings.

Fig Compote with Pears and Prosciutto

A wonderful dinner-party starter or luncheon dish.

⅓	cup brown sugar	75	mL
2	tablespoons white vinegar	25	mL
1	cup water	250	mL
½	teaspoon grated lemon rind	2	mL
2	teaspoons lemon juice	10	mL
1	cinnamon stick (2½"/6.5 cm)	1	
½	teaspoon ground ginger	2	mL
4	teaspoons chopped preserved ginger	20	mL
½	cup quartered dried figs	125	mL
3	ripe pears	3	
6	slices prosciutto	6	
	Basil or mint leaves for garnish		

Combine sugar, vinegar and water in a saucepan. Stir over medium heat, without boiling, until sugar is dissolved. Add lemon rind and juice, cinnamon, ground and preserved ginger and figs. Bring to a boil, reduce heat and simmer for about 40 minutes or until figs are tender. Let cool. Peel pears, slice in half and core. Cut into slices and arrange on salad plates with some fig compote and prosciutto. Garnish with basil or mint leaves.

Serves 6

Vegetable Tart

1	9" (23 cm) pastry shell, thawed, or your own pastry	1
1	package (8 oz/250 g) cream cheese, softened	1
½	cup mayonnaise	125 mL
½	teaspoon garlic salt	2 mL

Garnishes
Cherry tomatoes, halved
Mushrooms, sliced
Chopped fresh parsley
Ripe black olives, sliced

1	hard-boiled egg	1

Preheat oven to 425° F (220° C). On a large baking sheet, pat pastry into an 11" (28 cm) circle. Pierce with fork. Bake for 8 minutes until lightly browned. Cool. Carefully place pastry on serving dish. Beat cream cheese, mayonnaise and garlic salt together until smooth. Spread evenly on pastry. Cover. Chilled for up to 4 hours. Garnish just before serving by placing halved cherry tomatoes in a single row around the outside edge of pie. Place sliced white mushrooms in a circle next to the row of tomatoes. Next, place a band of chopped parsley. A band of sliced black olives is placed next to the parsley. Grate hard-boiled egg over the center of the pie. Cut into 12 wedges. Serve on a small plate with a fork as a starter.

Serves 12

Soups

Butternut Squash Soup with Ginger and Lime

½	cup chopped onion	125	mL
4	teaspoons minced peeled fresh ginger	20	mL
3	tablespoons unsalted butter	50	mL
4	cups peeled, seeded and thinly sliced butternut squash (about 1½ lb/750 g)	1	L
2	cups chicken broth	500	mL
2	cups water	500	mL
3	cloves garlic, minced	3	
2	tablespoons fresh lime juice	25	mL
	Salt and pepper to taste		

Garnish

2	tablespoons vegetable oil	25	mL
3	tablespoons julienne strips of peeled fresh ginger	50	mL
4-6	thin slices lime	4-6	

In a large saucepan, cook onion and ginger in butter over medium-low heat, stirring occasionally, until onion is soft. Add squash, chicken broth, water and garlic. Bring to a boil and simmer, covered, for 15 to 20 minutes or until squash is tender. Purée the mixture in batches in a blender or food processor. Return mixture to pan and stir in lime juice, salt and pepper. Reheat over moderate heat until hot. If soup is too thick, thin with a little chicken broth or water.

To make garnish, fry ginger strips in oil until pale golden and crisp. Drain on paper towel.

Serve soup in bowls. Float a slice of lime on each and top with fried ginger. Serve hot.

Serves 4 to 6

Parsnip and Carrot Soup

Unique and interesting flavor.

2	tablespoons butter	25	mL
3	carrots, peeled and chopped	3	
2	parsnips, peeled and chopped	2	
1	onion, peeled and chopped	1	
1	potato, peeled and chopped	1	
4	cups chicken stock	1	L
¼	cup 10% or 18% cream	50	mL
	Salt and pepper to taste		
	Chopped green onion or fresh parsley for garnish		

Melt butter in a saucepan; add carrots, parsnips, onion and potato. Cover and cook over low heat for 15 minutes. Stir in chicken stock and bring to a boil. Reduce heat and simmer for 30 minutes. In blender, blend mixture in small batches until smooth. Return to saucepan and stir in cream. Season to taste with salt and pepper. Reheat without boiling. Garnish individual servings with green onion or parsley. Delicious hot or cold.

Serves 4 to 6

Cajun Bouillabaisse
A meal in itself.

2	tablespoons olive or vegetable oil	25	mL
2-4	cloves garlic, minced	2-4	
1	sweet red pepper, chopped	1	
1	large onion, chopped	1	
1	can (28 oz/796 mL) tomatoes, with liquid, crushed	1	
1	bottle (8 oz/237 mL) clam juice	1	
½	teaspoon seafood seasoning	2	mL
¼	teaspoon black pepper	1	mL
¼	teaspoon hot pepper flakes	1	mL
2	bay leaves	2	
	Dash of hot pepper sauce		
2	tablespoons capers (optional)	25	mL
1½	pounds firm-fleshed fish (e.g., haddock, cod, monkfish), cut in bite-sized pieces	750	g
¼	cup chopped fresh parsley	50	mL

Using large saucepan, lightly sauté garlic, red pepper and onion in oil. Add tomatoes, clam juice, seafood seasoning, pepper, hot pepper flakes, bay leaves, hot pepper sauce and capers (if using). Bring to a boil and reduce heat to low; simmer, uncovered, for about 15 minutes or until sauce thickens. Remove bay leaves. (Recipe can be made ahead to this point and refrigerated for up to 2 days.) When ready to serve, add fish to simmering sauce; cook, without stirring, for approximately 5 minutes or until fish is cooked. Garnish with chopped parsley.

Serves 8

Blender Cucumber Soup

Delicious served cold on a summer day.

2	cups peeled, seeded and coarsely chopped cucumber	500	mL
1	cup chicken stock	250	mL
1	cup 10% cream	250	mL
2	tablespoons chopped fresh chives or 1 green onion, finely chopped	25	mL
¼	cup chopped celery leaves	50	mL
2	tablespoons butter, softened	25	mL
2	tablespoons all-purpose flour	25	mL
	Salt and pepper to taste		
	Sour cream and lime zest for garnish		

Place all ingredients except salt, pepper and garnish in a blender or food processor; whirl until smooth. Pour into a saucepan and cook over low heat for about 10 minutes, stirring constantly. Do not boil. Season with salt and pepper. If desired, thin with extra milk. Serve hot, or chill and serve cold. Garnish each bowl with a dollop of sour cream and a sprinkle of lime zest.

Serves 4

Chicken and Corn Soup

Feed a crowd or serve some of the soup now and freeze the rest for later.

1	chicken (3½ lb/1.75 kg)	1	
3	quarts water	3	L
1	large onion, diced	1	
2	stalks celery, chopped	2	
1	teaspoon pepper	5	mL
2-3	tablespoons powdered chicken stock	25-50	mL
½	teaspoon celery seed	2	mL
2½	cups corn kernels	625	mL
1	can (19 oz/540 mL) creamed corn	1	
1	can (10 oz/284 mL) cream of celery soup	1	

Dough Balls

1	cup all-purpose flour	250	mL
¼	teaspoon salt	1	mL
¼	teaspoon baking powder	1	mL
1	egg	1	

Using a large pot, cover chicken with water; add onion, celery, pepper, powdered chicken stock and celery seed. Bring to a boil; lower heat and simmer, covered, for 2 hours or until chicken is tender. Remove chicken from pot, reserving broth. Discard skin and bones; dice meat. Skim fat from top of broth. This is easier if allowed to solidify in refrigerator. When this step is completed, add chicken, corn kernels, creamed corn and celery soup to pot of broth. In a separate bowl, prepare dough balls by combining flour, salt and baking powder. Add egg and mix thoroughly. Bring soup to a boil. While stirring boiling soup, hold crumbly dough-ball mixture in the palm of your hand (palm up) and gently shake through your fingers. This will have the appearance of very tiny dumplings. Reduce heat and simmer for about 15 minutes.

Serves 12 generously

Chunky Pizza Soup
A hearty winter lunch.

1	tablespoon vegetable oil	15	mL
1	small onion, chopped	1	
½	cup sliced mushrooms	125	mL
¼	cup julienne sweet green pepper	50	mL
1	can (28 oz/796 mL) tomatoes	1	
1	cup beef broth	250	mL
1	cup thinly sliced pepperoni	250	mL
½	teaspoon dried basil	2	mL
	Crusty French bread slices, toasted		
1	cup shredded mozzarella cheese	250	mL
	Grated Parmesan cheese		

Heat oil in a large saucepan. Sauté onion, mushrooms and green pepper briefly. Stir in tomatoes, beef broth, pepperoni and basil. Cook until heated through. Ladle soup into 4 onion soup bowls; place bread slices on top. Mound mozzarella over bread; sprinkle with Parmesan. Broil until cheese melts.

Serves 4

* Sauté 1 minced clove of garlic along with the onion, mushrooms and green pepper. Change the pepperoni to sliced sweet or hot cooked Italian sausage. Double the basil quantity. Add some oregano, too, if you like.

Mexican Squash Soup

For those nippy fall days. This is also delicious made with pumpkin.

3	cups peeled and cubed squash (butternut, buttercup or Hubbard)	750	mL
5-6	cups water or chicken stock	1.25-1.5	L
2	tablespoons butter	25	mL
1	cup chopped onions	250	mL
1	teaspoon ground cumin	5	mL
1¼	teaspoons chili powder	6	mL
½	teaspoon cinnamon	2	mL
¼	teaspoon ground nutmeg	1	mL
	Pinch of ground allspice		
1	tablespoon grated fresh ginger	15	mL
1	cup 10% cream or milk	250	mL
	Chopped fresh parsley or coriander for garnish		

Boil squash in water or stock until very tender. Purée squash and liquid in batches in a blender or food processor. In a large saucepan, melt butter; sauté onions until soft. Add spices and ginger; cook for 1 minute longer to release flavors. Add squash purée to this mixture; simmer over low heat for 20 minutes. (Soup can be prepared ahead to this point and refrigerated.) Just before serving, add cream or milk; heat gently. Do not boil. Garnish with fresh parsley or coriander.

Serves 8

Carrot-Orange Soup with Yogurt Garnish

A tasty blend of hot and cold.

¼	cup butter	50	mL
2	cups finely chopped onions	500	mL
5	cups sliced carrots	1.25	L
4	cups chicken stock	1	L
1	cup fresh orange juice	250	mL
2	teaspoons grated orange rind	10	mL
2	tablespoons orange juice concentrate	25	mL
	(or more to taste)		
	Salt and pepper to taste		
	Plain yogurt for garnish		

Melt butter in a large soup pot. Add onions; cover and cook over low heat for about 25 minutes. Add carrots and stock; bring to a boil. Reduce heat and cook until carrots are very tender. Purée in batches in blender or food processor until smooth. Return purée to pot. Add orange juice, rind, concentrate, salt and pepper. Dilute with more chicken stock if necessary and simmer until heated through. Garnish each bowl with a dollop of yogurt.

Serves 8 to 10

Mexican Rice and Bean Soup
A hearty winter soup.

1	pound pork sausage or bulk sausage	500	g
1	tablespoon oil	15	mL
½	cup chopped onions	125	mL
⅓	cup chopped sweet green pepper	75	mL
1	clove garlic, minced	1	
3	cups water	750	mL
1	can (19 oz/540 mL) tomato juice	1	
1	can (19 oz/540 mL) kidney beans	1	
½	cup long-grain rice	125	mL
1	teaspoon paprika	5	mL
½-1	teaspoon chili powder	2-5	mL
	Salt and pepper to taste		

Cut sausage into bite-sized pieces or break up bulk sausage. Using a large saucepan, lightly brown sausage in oil. Spoon off all but 2 tablespoons (25 mL) of the fat. Add onions, green pepper and garlic. Cook until vegetables are tender but not brown. Add water, tomato juice, beans, rice and spices. Simmer, covered, for 20 to 30 minutes or until rice is tender. Stir occasionally. This soup freezes well.

Serves 6 to 8

Watercress Soup
Smooth and creamy!

¼	cup unsalted butter	50	mL
2	onions, sliced	2	
2	stalks celery, thinly sliced	2	
4	potatoes, peeled and diced	4	
6	cups chicken broth	1.5	L
2	cups watercress leaves	500	mL
	Salt and pepper to taste		
2	cups 10% cream	500	mL

Using a large saucepan, sauté onions and celery in butter until soft. Add potatoes and chicken broth; simmer until potatoes are completely tender. Stir in watercress; cook for 1 to 2 minutes or until wilted. Cool soup slightly. Purée in batches in blender or food processor. For a very smooth soup, strain through a sieve. Season with salt and pepper. Just before serving, stir in cream. Do not boil after adding cream. Soup may be served hot or cold.

Serves 10

Venetian Vegetable Soup

Chop your way to a succulent soup.

¼	cup olive oil	50 mL
2	onions, chopped	2
4	tomatoes, peeled and chopped	4
½	cucumber, seeded and chopped	½
5	potatoes, cubed	5
2	stalks celery, chopped	2
4	leeks (white part only), chopped or julienne	4
2	carrots, julienne	2
½	cauliflower, chopped	½
½	cabbage, shredded	½
4	zucchini, sliced	4
2	bay leaves	2
2	fresh thyme sprigs, chopped	2
3	fresh parsley sprigs, chopped	3
8	fresh basil leaves, chopped	8
8	cups chicken or beef broth	2 L
	Salt and pepper to taste	
	Grated Parmesan or mozzarella cheese for garnish	

In a large pot, heat oil over medium heat and sauté onions until soft. Add tomatoes and cucumber; cook for 5 minutes. Add remaining vegetables, bay leaves, thyme, parsley and basil. Simmer, stirring occasionally, for about 20 minutes or until vegetables are tender-crisp. Stir in broth, salt and pepper; heat through. Remove bay leaves. Serve with grated Parmesan or mozzarella cheese.

Serves 8 to 10

Guilt-Free Soup

A meal in a bowl.

1	cup any small- to medium-sized pasta	250	mL
1	tablespoon olive oil	15	mL
1-2	large cloves garlic, minced	1-2	
1	large onion, chopped	1	
3	stalks celery, diagonally sliced	3	
1	sweet pepper (any color), chopped	1	
1	tablespoon Beau Monde seasoning or seasoning salt	15	mL
1	can (19 oz/540 mL) tomatoes	1	
3	cups chicken broth	750	mL
12	mushrooms, quartered	12	
1	cup cauliflower florets	250	mL
¼	cup chopped fresh basil (or 1 tablespoon/15 mL dried)	50	mL
¼	cup chopped fresh parsley	50	mL
2	small zucchini, diagonally sliced	2	
	Freshly ground pepper		
1	tablespoon fresh lemon juice	15	mL
	Freshly grated Parmesan cheese (optional)		

Cook the pasta in boiling, salted water until al dente. Drain and set aside. Heat oil in a large saucepan. Sauté garlic, onion and celery over medium heat for 5 minutes or until soft but not brown. Add sweet pepper; sauté for 3 minutes longer. Add Beau Monde, tomatoes and chicken broth. Bring to a simmer and cook for 15 to 20 minutes. Add mushrooms, cauliflower, basil and parsley. Simmer for 10 minutes. Add zucchini; cook just until tender. Add pepper, lemon juice and cooked pasta. Pass Parmesan cheese separately at the table if desired.

Serves 4 to 6

Tomato Tarragon Soup

We like it hot. Some like it cold – delicious either way!

1	tablespoon olive oil	15	mL
1	pound cooking onions, sliced	500	g
3	cloves garlic, minced	3	
1	can (28 oz/796 mL) tomatoes (or 3 pounds/1.5 kg fresh tomatoes, peeled)	1	
3	tablespoons dried tarragon	50	mL
5	cups chicken broth	1.25	L
¼	teaspoon dried thyme	1	mL
¼	teaspoon dried oregano	1	mL
½	teaspoon dried parsley	2	mL
½	teaspoon dried basil	2	mL
2	tablespoons sugar	25	mL
3	bay leaves	3	
	Dash of Worcestershire sauce		
	Dash of hot pepper sauce		
	Salt and pepper to taste		

Heat oil in a large saucepan over medium heat. Sauté the onions and garlic until soft but not browned. Add tomatoes and tarragon; continue to sauté for about 2 minutes. Add chicken broth and the remaining ingredients; bring to a boil. Reduce heat; simmer, uncovered, for about 40 minutes. Remove bay leaves. Purée mixture in batches in food processor or blender. Serve hot or cold.

Serves 6

Brandied Chestnut Soup

A rich and elegant soup for festive occasions.

2	tablespoons butter or margarine	25	mL
½	cup finely chopped onion	125	mL
1	large clove garlic, minced	1	
3½	cups chicken broth	875	mL
1½	pound unshelled chestnuts [or 1 can (15 oz/435 g) unsweetened chestnut purée]	750	g
3	tablespoons brandy	50	mL
½	teaspoon salt	2	mL
¼	teaspoon brown sugar	1	mL
	Pinch of cayenne pepper (optional)		
1	cup 10% cream	250	mL
	Milk		

In a large saucepan, melt butter. Add onion and garlic; sauté until soft.
Add chicken broth, prepared chestnuts (see note below) or purée, brandy,
salt, sugar and cayenne pepper. Bring to a boil. Reduce heat; simmer,
covered, for approximately 30 to 35 minutes. Purée mixture, in batches,
in blender or food processor. Return to pan; stir in cream. Heat until hot,
but do not boil. Thin to desired consistency with a little milk.

Serves 6

* To prepare chestnuts, slash each nut with a sharp knife. Place nuts in a
saucepan and cover with cold water. Bring to a boil; simmer for 3 to 5
minutes. Drain and let stand until cool enough to handle. Cut each
chestnut in half and scoop out the center. Discard the skin and shell.

Bountiful Bean Soup

1¼	cups mixed dried beans	300	mL
	(¼ cup/50 mL of any 5 of the following: navy beans, red kidney beans, black beans, black-eyed peas, lentils, split green or yellow peas, barley, pinto beans or romano beans)		
8	cups water	2	L
1	pork hock (available in delicatessens or most supermarkets)	1	
1	package (1.8 oz/45 g) onion soup mix	1	
1	package (1.8 oz/45 g) vegetable soup mix	1	
1	clove garlic, minced	1	
1	sweet red pepper, chopped	1	
1	sweet green pepper, chopped	1	
3	stalks celery including leaves, chopped	3	
1	cup sliced carrots	250	mL
1	can (28 oz/796 mL) tomatoes	1	
	Black pepper to taste		

Wash and soak beans overnight. Drain and place in a large saucepan with the water. Add pork hock, soup mixes and garlic. Simmer, covered, for 2 hours. Lift pork hock from broth. Discard skin and bones and return meat to saucepan. Add remaining ingredients; simmer, covered, for 30 minutes or until vegetables are tender.

Serves approximately 10

* To add more meat to your meal, try 1 pound (500 g) cooked, sliced sausage. Stir in during the final 5 minutes of cooking.

* For an attractive gift, carefully layer a jar with several varieties of the beans. Use ¼ cup (50 mL) beans for each layer. Top jar with a fabric bonnet and attach the recipe.

Salads

Warm Ginger Chicken Salad

If you've never tried a warm salad, try this one!

2	half chicken breasts, boned and skinned	2
1	sweet red pepper, julienne	1
½	pound slim asparagus, diagonally sliced and blanched for 1 minute	250 g
1	grapefruit, peeled, sectioned and membranes removed	1
½	cup unsalted cashews, toasted	125 mL
	Mixture of assorted greens (Boston lettuce, radicchio, Belgian endive, etc.), washed and torn, or left in whole leaves to serve 4	

Dressing

2	tablespoons coarsely chopped Spanish onion	25 mL
1	piece (approximately 1½"/4 cm long) fresh ginger, peeled	1
1	teaspoon Dijon mustard, or more to taste	5 mL
2	tablespoons rice vinegar	25 mL
1	teaspoon honey	5 mL
	Salt to taste	
¼	cup olive oil	50 mL

To make dressing, in a food processor or by hand, chop onion and fresh ginger finely. Add mustard, rice vinegar, honey, and salt; blend. Drizzle in oil while blending. Set aside.

Slice chicken into ½" x 2" (1.5 cm x 5 cm) pieces. Place in a ceramic bowl; spoon approximately 2 tablespoons (25 mL) of the dressing over chicken. Toss to coat. Marinate for 1 to 2 hours at room temperature. Just before serving, arrange prepared lettuces on 4 individual plates or on a platter. Heat a fry pan over medium-high heat; add chicken. Toss and sauté until cooked. Remove from pan. Add red pepper, asparagus and grapefruit to fry pan; sauté until hot. Add chicken, cashews and remaining dressing to pan. Heat until warmed through. Spoon over greens. Serve immediately.

Serves 4

Warm Salad with Shrimp, Chicken or Scallops

2	tablespoons olive oil	25	mL
1	pound large shrimps or scallops (halved) or boneless chicken (cut in strips)	500	g
	Salt and pepper to taste		
	Mixed greens (Boston lettuce, arugula, or Belgian endive), washed and torn in bite-sized pieces		
2	tablespoons minced fresh herbs (parsley, chervil, tarragon and/or dill)	25	mL
½	cup julienne carrots	125	mL
½	cup julienne celery	125	mL
½	cup julienne sweet red pepper	125	mL

Dressing

½	cup olive oil	125	mL
¼	cup balsamic vinegar	50	mL
1	tablespoon Dijon mustard	15	mL
1	clove garlic, minced	1	

Heat the 2 tablespoons (25 mL) oil in a skillet over medium-high heat. Add shrimps; cook, stirring frequently, until cooked but not dry. Season with salt and pepper. Drain on paper towel; keep warm. Add the ½ cup oil, vinegar, mustard and garlic to the drippings in the skillet; cook, stirring, for 1 minute over low heat.

Arrange prepared salad greens on salad plates. Sprinkle with herbs. Top with carrots, celery and pepper. Arrange warm shrimp over vegetables; drizzle with warm dressing. Serve immediately.

Serves 6

Beet and Orange Salad

This is a wonderful winter salad. For added color, use one Italian blood orange.

2	large navel oranges	2
1	can (19 oz/540 mL) sliced beets, drained	1
1	large red onion, sliced	1
2	large stalks celery, sliced on diagonal	2
	Lettuce leaves to line bowl	
2	tablespoons chopped pecans for garnish	25 mL

Dressing

½	cup olive oil	125 mL
¼	cup red wine vinegar	50 mL
2	teaspoons water or orange juice	10 mL
1	tablespoon orange rind, grated	15 mL
1	teaspoon brown sugar	5 mL
½	teaspoon salt	2 mL

Peel oranges, carefully removing all white membrane; cut into thin slices. Layer oranges, beets, onion and celery in a bowl. Combine dressing ingredients in a covered jar; shake to mix well. Pour dressing over layered fruit and vegetables. Cover and refrigerate. Serve in a salad bowl or on individual plates lined with lettuce leaves. Sprinkle with pecans.

Serves 6

Watercress Salad

A light and luscious salad.

2	bunches watercress	2
2	navel oranges, peeled, sectioned and membrane removed	2
1	red onion, sliced	1
½	cup pine nuts, lightly toasted	125 mL
	Salt and pepper to taste	

Dressing

½	cup olive oil	125 mL
2	tablespoons wine vinegar	25 mL
1	teaspoon Dijon mustard	5 mL

Trim tough ends off watercress stems and discard. Wash and dry watercress. Place orange pieces, onion and pine nuts in salad bowl. Combine dressing ingredients; pour over orange mixture. Just before serving, toss in watercress. Season with salt and pepper.

Serves 6

Belgian Endive and Bacon Salad

6	heads Belgian endive	6	
8	slices bacon	8	
2	tablespoons chopped fresh parsley	25	mL
2	shallots, chopped	2	

Dressing

¼	cup walnut oil	50	mL
¼	cup olive oil	50	mL
¼	cup white wine vinegar	50	mL
	Salt to taste		
	Pinch of sugar or to taste		
	Freshly ground black pepper		

Wash endive; trim outer leaves. Cut ½" (1.5 cm) off bottoms; then cut in half lengthwise. Slice halves into julienne strips. Cut bacon across the strips into ⅛" (3 mm) pieces; sauté over medium heat until almost crisp. Drain on paper towel. To make the dressing, whisk oils into vinegar. Add salt and sugar to taste. Whisk to dissolve. Toss the salad ingredients with enough dressing to moisten. Grind pepper over all.

Serves 6 to 8

Chicken-Cabbage Salad

A crunchy salad with a taste of the Orient.

4	half chicken breasts, cooked and cut in julienne strips	4	
4	cups red or green shredded cabbage	1	L
1	package (3 oz/85 g) Japanese noodle soup mix, any flavor (use noodles only and do not cook)	1	
4	green onions, sliced thinly	4	
½	cup slivered almonds, toasted	125	mL
¼	cup sesame seeds, toasted	50	mL

Dressing

2	tablespoons sugar	25	mL
1½-2	teaspoons pepper	7-10	mL
⅓	cup vegetable oil	75	mL
½	teaspoon salt	2	mL
3	tablespoons white wine vinegar	50	mL
1	teaspoon sesame oil	5	mL

Mix all dressing ingredients together in a jar. Shake to combine. Let stand for 2 hours to blend flavors. At serving time, combine chicken, cabbage, noodles, green onions, almonds and sesame seeds in a salad bowl. Toss with dressing. Noodles will lose their crunch if allowed to stand.

Serves 6

* You may add the seasoning package from the noodles to the dressing, if you wish.

Chick-Pea Salad

Quick and nutritious – good too!

2	cans (each 19 oz/540 mL) chick-peas	2
1	sweet red pepper, julienne	1
1	green pepper, julienne	1
2	green onions, diagonally sliced	2

Dressing

½	cup vegetable oil	125	mL
3	tablespoons freshly squeezed lemon juice	50	mL
2	cloves garlic, minced	2	
	Dash of hot pepper sauce		
¼	teaspoon chili powder	1	mL
	Generous pinches of salt and pepper		

Drain and rinse chick-peas. Combine with red and green peppers and green onions in a bowl. In a separate bowl, whisk together all dressing ingredients. Toss salad with dressing; refrigerate until ready to serve. Flavor improves if left to marinate overnight.

Serves 6 to 8

Three-Potato Salad

Just when you thought there was nothing new in potato salads.

3	red potatoes	3	
2-3	sweet potatoes	2-3	
3	white potatoes	3	
2	green onions, diagonally sliced	2	
⅓	cup diced red onions	75	mL
¼	cup snipped fresh chives	50	mL
	Salt and freshly ground pepper to taste		
⅔	cup mayonnaise	150	mL
⅓	cup light or regular sour cream	75	mL
1	teaspoon Dijon mustard	5	mL
1	teaspoon honey mustard	5	mL
½	teaspoon prepared mustard	2	mL
8	slices bacon, cooked crisp and crumbled	8	
1	cup frozen small peas, defrosted (no need to cook)	250	mL

Cook unpeeled potatoes in boiling, salted water just until tender. Do not overcook. Drain, cool and peel. (If using small new red and white potatoes, they do not need to be peeled.) Cut into ½" (1.5 cm) cubes. In a bowl, place potatoes, onions, chives, salt and pepper. Mix mayonnaise, sour cream and mustards together. Toss potato mixture with enough dressing to moisten. Save any remaining dressing in case more is needed at serving time. Add crumbled bacon and peas. Toss again gently. Refrigerate several hours to blend flavors. Serve chilled.

Serves 6 to 10

Shrimp, Mango and Avocado Salad

2	avocados, cubed	2
2	mangoes, cubed	2
1	pound large shrimps, cooked, shelled and deveined	500 g
½	pound mushrooms, cleaned and sliced	250 g

Dressing

1	teaspoon fresh ginger juice (see note below)	5 mL
½	cup vegetable oil	125 mL
2	tablespoons white vinegar	25 mL
1	tablespoon lemon juice	15 mL
1½	teaspoons honey	7 mL
1	teaspoon grainy Dijon mustard	5 mL
1	tablespoon chopped fresh chives	15 mL
1	teaspoon chopped fresh dill	5 mL

Place avocados, mangoes, shrimps and mushrooms in a glass salad bowl.

To make dressing, combine all dressing ingredients and shake well. Toss salad with dressing just before serving.

Serves 6

* To make ginger juice, press peeled ginger through a garlic press.

* Serve in avocado shells as a starter or a luncheon dish.

* Toss salad with 1 head of Boston lettuce torn in bite-sized pieces.

Sweet and Nutty Broccoli Salad
Triples and quadruples beautifully for a crowd!

Dressing

1½	cups mayonnaise	375	mL
2	tablespoons wine vinegar	25	mL
1	tablespoon Dijon mustard	15	mL
3	tablespoons honey	50	mL
½	cup raisins	125	mL

Salad

2	bunches broccoli (tips only), cut in florets	2	
1	red onion, chopped	1	
1	cup sunflower seeds or pine nuts	250	mL
¼	pound bacon, cooked and crumbled	125	g

To make dressing, combine mayonnaise, vinegar, mustard and honey. Add raisins and let stand for at least 30 minutes. The flavors blend even better if allowed to stand, refrigerated, overnight. Just before serving, combine salad ingredients; toss with dressing, so that dressing lightly coats broccoli, saving any extra dressing for another use.

Serves 8

Hearts of Palm and Artichoke Salad

This is a delicious make-ahead salad.

1	can (14 oz/398 mL) hearts of palm	1
1	can (14 oz/398 mL) artichoke hearts	1
¼	sweet red pepper, julienne	¼
2	tablespoons chopped fresh parsley	25 mL
	Boston lettuce	

Dressing
¼	cup raspberry vinegar	50 mL
1	tablespoon Dijon mustard	15 mL
⅔	cup walnut oil	150 mL
	Salt to taste	
	Freshly ground black pepper	

Drain, rinse and cut hearts of palm and artichoke hearts into bite-sized pieces; place in a bowl. Add red pepper and parsley; set aside. In a small bowl, whisk together vinegar and mustard. Gradually add oil, whisking until thickened. Season with salt and pepper; pour over salad. Marinate for 3 to 4 hours or overnight. Serve on Boston lettuce leaves.

Serves 6 to 8

Avocado and Papaya Salad
Two of our favorite things combined in a salad.

2	heads Boston lettuce, washed and torn	2
1	papaya, peeled and chopped (reserve seeds for dressing)	1
1	avocado, peeled and chopped	1
4-6	green onions, chopped	4-6

Dressing

½	cup vegetable oil	125	mL
½	cup vinegar	125	mL
½	cup granulated sugar	125	mL
2	teaspoons dry mustard	10	mL
1	teaspoon salt	5	mL
2	tablespoons papaya seeds	25	mL

In a large salad bowl, combine lettuce, papaya, avocado and green onions. Combine all dressing ingredients in blender or food processor, blending until papaya seeds are slightly crushed. Pour dressing over salad; toss gently. Serve immediately.

Serves 4 to 6

Couscous Salad

A refreshing new taste.

1½	cups water	375 mL
1	cup couscous	250 mL
½	cup raisins	125 mL
1	can (19 oz/540 mL) chick-peas, rinsed and drained	1
3-4	green onions, chopped	3-4
1	sweet red pepper, diced	1
1	zucchini, diced	1
¼	cup chopped fresh parsley	50 mL
⅓	cup diced, dried papaya or apricots	75 mL

Dressing

3	tablespoons fresh lemon juice	50 mL
1	clove garlic, minced	1
	Salt and pepper to taste	
½-1	teaspoon ground cumin	2-5 mL
¼-½	teaspoon turmeric	1-2 mL
	Dash of hot pepper sauce	
½	cup olive or vegetable oil	125 mL

Bring the water to a boil; pour 1 cup (250 mL) of the boiled water over couscous in a medium bowl. Pour the remaining ½ cup (125 mL) water over the raisins in a small bowl. Let each stand for 30 minutes. Couscous will absorb all the water. Stir to break grains apart. Drain the raisins; add to couscous along with chick-peas, green onions, red pepper, zucchini, parsley and papaya. Toss gently.

In a small bowl, whisk together dressing ingredients; pour over salad. Toss. Chill to let flavors blend. Can be made a day in advance.

Serves 8

Italian Cabbage Salad

Bellissima!

½	small red cabbage	½	
½	small green cabbage	½	
2	large cloves garlic, minced	2	
1	can (2 oz/50 g) anchovy fillets	1	
1	tablespoon wine vinegar	15	mL
½	cup olive or vegetable oil	125	mL
	Salt and freshly ground black pepper		
	Parsley sprigs for garnish		

Core cabbages, cut into very thin slices and place in two separate bowls. Combine garlic and undrained anchovies; mash into a paste. Stir in vinegar, oil, salt and pepper. (Do not use a food processor, as dressing will become too thick.) Dressing should remain a clear vinaigrette to enhance the colors of the salad. Divide the dressing between the two bowls of cabbage, keeping the colors separate until serving time.

At serving time, place green cabbage in glass bowl. Make a neat well in the center. Fill with the red cabbage, mounding attractively. Keep the two colors of cabbage distinctly separate. Garnish around the rim of the bowl with parsley. This salad is best served the day it is made.

Serves 6

Leeks in Tarragon Dressing

10	small to medium-sized leeks	10
4	cups water	1 L
3	tablespoons white wine vinegar	50 mL
1	tablespoon lemon juice	15 mL
1	teaspoon Dijon mustard	5 mL
1	egg yolk	1
¼	cup fresh tarragon leaves	50 mL
¼	cup chopped fresh parsley	50 mL
1	clove garlic, minced	1
¼	teaspoon salt	1 mL
	Pinch of pepper	
¼	cup olive oil	50 mL
½	cup salad oil	125 mL
⅓	cup red and yellow bell pepper strips, 1½" (4 cm) long	75 mL
2	tablespoons chopped fresh chives	15 mL

Trim leeks, discarding coarse outer leaves. Cut in half lengthwise. Hold each half under cold running water, separating layers gently to rinse out dirt, but leaving them intact. Place leeks in a single layer in a large skillet; add the 4 cups (1 L) water to cover. Bring to boil over high heat; reduce heat. Simmer, covered, until stem ends are tender, appoximately 5 minutes. Lift leeks out and let cool to room temperature.

In a blender or food processor, combine vinegar, lemon juice, mustard, egg yolk, tarragon, parsley, garlic, salt and pepper. Mix at high speed until tarragon and parsley are puréed. Add olive oil and salad oil; whirl until oil is incorporated. Cover and refrigerate, if made ahead. Place 3 to 4 tablespoons (50 mL) of the dressing on each individual salad plate. Arrange leek halves on plates; sprinkle with bell peppers and chives. Serve immediately.

Serves 6

Oriental Vegetable Salad

This salad is best made the day before.

Salad

1	can (8 oz/227 mL) miniature corn cobs, chopped	1
1	can (10 oz/284 mL) petits pois (tiny peas)	1
2	cans (each 10 oz/284 mL) sliced water chestnuts	2
1	jar (4 ½ oz/128 mL) pimientos, sliced	1
1	pound fresh bean sprouts	500 g
1	sweet green pepper, julienne	1
1	cup julienne celery	250 mL
1	cup sliced fresh mushrooms	250 mL
3	green onions, chopped	3
	Fresh spinach to line bowl	

Marinade

1	cup light salad oil	250 mL
½	cup vinegar (cider, red wine or rice)	125 mL
½	cup water	125 mL
2	tablespoons dry mustard	25 mL
¾	cup granulated sugar	175 mL

Drain liquid from corn, peas, water chestnuts and pimientos. In a large bowl, combine drained vegetables with bean sprouts, green pepper, celery, mushrooms and green onions. Place marinade ingredients in a jar; shake well. Add marinade to vegetables; mix gently. Refrigerate for at least 24 hours. Drain marinade; serve salad in a glass bowl lined with spinach leaves.

Serves 10 to 12

Zucchini Mint Salad

A fresh-tasting, minty salad – the perfect accompaniment to lamb.

4-6	cups fresh spinach, torn	1-1.5	L
1-2	zucchini, cut into bite-sized pieces	1-2	
½	red onion, sliced	½	
¾	cup crumbled feta cheese	175	mL

Dressing

⅔	cup olive oil	150	mL
3	tablespoons bottled mint sauce	50	mL
2	tablespoons fresh lime juice	25	mL
1	teaspoon Dijon mustard	5	mL
1	clove garlic, minced	1	
¼	cup chopped fresh mint	50	mL
	Pepper to taste		

In a large salad bowl, combine spinach, zucchini, onion and feta cheese. Combine dressing ingredients in a jar; shake well. Toss with salad just before serving.

Serves 6 to 8

Spinach, Kiwi and Strawberry Salad

If spinach isn't your favorite, try watercress.

2	bunches spinach, washed and torn	2	
2	kiwis, peeled and sliced	2	
1	quart strawberries, hulled and sliced	1	L

Dressing

2	tablespoons sesame seeds	25	mL
1	tablespoon poppy seeds	15	mL
¼	cup cider vinegar	50	mL
¼	cup granulated sugar	50	mL
½	cup salad oil	125	mL
1	teaspoon Worcestershire sauce	5	mL
½	teaspoon paprika	2	mL
4	teaspoons minced onion	20	mL

Combine dressing ingredients together in a jar. Cover and shake well. Let stand to blend flavors. At serving time, place spinach in a salad bowl. Add kiwis and strawberries. Toss with dressing.

Serves 10

Greek Garlic Chicken Salad

Jumping with garlic flavor.

3	cups cooked chicken, cut in ¾" (2 cm) cubes	750	mL
1¼	cups crumbled feta cheese	300	mL
⅔	cup ripe black olives, pitted	150	mL
¼	cup chopped fresh parsley	50	mL
1	teaspoon dried oregano (optional)	5	mL
2	cups peeled, seeded and diced cucumber	500	mL
½	cup yogurt	125	mL
	Lettuce leaves		

Dressing

3	cloves garlic, minced	3	
1	cup mayonnaise	250	mL

In a bowl, combine chicken, feta, olives, parsley and oregano (if using). For dressing, combine garlic and mayonnaise; stir into chicken mixture. Let stand for 1 hour in refrigerator to develop flavors. Just before serving, fold in cucumber and yogurt. Serve on a bed of lettuce.

Serves 4 to 6

Casual Fare

Tomato-Cheese Pie with Crumb Crust

1	cup fresh bread crumbs	250	mL
3	tablespoons butter or margarine, melted	50	mL
3	tablespoons grated Swiss cheese	50	mL
2	large firm tomatoes, sliced	2	
½	teaspoon granulated sugar	2	mL
	Salt and pepper to taste		
½	teaspoon dried basil	2	mL
2	green onions, chopped	2	
2	eggs, beaten	2	
½	cup 10% cream	125	mL
½	cup grated Swiss cheese	125	mL

Preheat oven to 400° F (200° C). Combine crumbs, butter and the 3 tablespoons (50 mL) cheese. Pat into greased 9" (23 cm) pie plate; bake for 10 minutes. Remove from oven. Lower oven temperature to 350° F (180° C). Spread tomatoes in a layer on pie crust. Sprinkle with sugar, salt, pepper, basil and green onions. Mix eggs with cream and the ½ cup (125 mL) cheese; pour over tomatoes. Bake for 30 minutes.

Serves 6

Cauliflower-Cheese Pie with Potato Crust

Crust

2	cups packed, grated raw potatoes	500	mL
½	teaspoon salt	2	mL
1	egg, beaten	1	
¼	cup grated onion	50	mL

Filling

1	cup chopped onions	250	mL
1	clove garlic, minced	1	
3	tablespoons butter	50	mL
½	teaspoon salt	2	mL
1	cauliflower, broken into small florets	1	
	Pinch of thyme		
½	teaspoon dried basil	2	mL
1	heaping packed cup of grated Cheddar cheese	250	mL
3	eggs	3	
⅓	cup milk	75	mL
	Pinch of black pepper		
	Pinch of paprika		

Preheat oven to 400° F (200° C). Put freshly grated potatoes in a colander over a bowl. Salt potatoes; drain for 10 minutes. Squeeze out excess moisture. In bowl, combine potatoes with egg and grated onion. Pat into a well-greased 9" (23 cm) pie plate. Build up sides of crust, using slightly floured fingers. Bake for 30 minutes. Brush the crust lightly with oil and bake for a further 15 minutes or until browned. Remove from oven. Reduce heat to 375° F (190° C). In a large fry pan, lightly sauté onions and garlic in butter and salt for 5 minutes. Add cauliflower and herbs. Cook, covered, for about 10 minutes, stirring occasionally. Spread half of the cheese on top of baked crust. Cover with cauliflower mixture; top with remaining cheese. In a separate bowl, beat eggs, milk and pepper. Pour over pie; sprinkle with paprika. Bake for 30 minutes or until set.

Serves 6 to 8

Baked Pork with Apples and Sweet Potatoes

Wonderful as a buffet casserole for a party.

2	pounds lean pork (leg or loin), cut into chunks	1	kg
5	tablespoons all-purpose flour	75	mL
1	tablespoon vegetable oil	15	mL
2	tablespoons butter	25	mL
1	onion, cut into chunks	1	
4	cooking apples, peeled, cored, quartered and sliced	4	
4-5	cups pure unsweetened apple cider	1-1.25	L
4	chicken bouillon cubes	4	
1	tablespoon Dijon mustard	15	mL
3-4	sweet potatoes, peeled and cubed Freshly ground black pepper	3-4	

Preheat oven to 325° F (160° C). Place pork chunks and flour into a plastic bag; shake to coat pork thoroughly. Heat oil and butter in a heavy fry pan. Add pork; sauté until brown, adding onion during the last few minutes. Remove pork and onion to a shallow casserole dish. Lightly sauté apples in the fry pan. Apples should remain slightly crunchy. Remove from pan and set aside. Pour apple cider into pan; stir to scrape up any browned bits. Add chicken bouillon cubes and Dijon mustard. Heat and stir until cubes have dissolved and mixture is hot. Pour cider mixture over pork and onion, making sure that meat is at least ¾ covered. Add more cider if necessary. Cover tightly and bake for 1½ hours. Add sweet potatoes and pepper to casserole; cover and bake for 20 minutes or until potatoes are tender. Add apple slices.

Serves 6 to 8

Original Canadian Tourtière
Always a favorite!

½	pound ground pork	250	g
½	pound ground veal	250	g
⅓	cup chopped onion	75	mL
⅓	cup water	75	mL
¼	teaspoon white pepper	1	mL
1	teaspoon salt	5	mL
¼	teaspoon ground cloves	1	mL
¼	teaspoon cinnamon	1	mL
¼	teaspoon celery salt	1	mL
¼	teaspoon savory	1	mL
1-2	potatoes, boiled and mashed	1-2	
1	pastry for 8" (20 cm) double-crust pie	1	

Preheat oven to 425° F (220° C). Place pork, veal, onion and water in a saucepan. Simmer until color changes. Add seasonings; simmer for a little longer. Thoroughly drain meat. Mix in mashed potatoes. Fit bottom pastry into 8" (20 cm) pie plate. Fill with meat mixture. Cover with top crust. Seal edges as desired and vent top to allow steam to escape. Bake for 10 minutes; lower oven temperature to 400° F (200° C) and bake for 20 to 25 minutes or until crust is golden brown and filling is hot.

Serves 6

* Serve with our Spiced Grapes (page 196), Tomato Butter (page 197) or Mother's Red and Green Tomato Chow Chow (page 200).

* If you like your tourtière spicy, by all means increase the seasonings to your taste.

Salmagundi

A variation of an old English supper dish.

Meatballs

1½	pounds ground beef	750	g
¼	cup chopped onion	50	mL
½	cup bread crumbs	125	mL
2	eggs	2	
1	tablespoon chili powder	15	mL
1	teaspoon Worcestershire sauce	5	mL
	Salt to taste		
	Pepper to taste		
1	can (28 oz/796 mL) spaghetti sauce	1	

Casserole

4	onions, sliced in rings	4	
3	tablespoons butter or vegetable oil	50	mL
½	cup dark brown sugar	125	mL
¼	cup molasses	50	mL
1	tablespoon dry hot mustard	15	mL
1	can (28 oz/796 mL) beans with pork	1	
1	can (28 oz/796 mL) kidney beans, drained	1	
1	can (19 oz/540 mL) lima beans, drained	1	

Preheat broiler. Combine the first eight ingredients; form into meatballs. Place on a cookie sheet; broil to brown. Remove from oven. Reduce heat to 350° F (180° C). Pour spaghetti sauce into a saucepan. Using a slotted spoon, transfer meat balls to the spaghetti sauce; simmer for 15 minutes. Meanwhile, in a large fry pan, sauté sliced onions in butter until translucent. Add brown sugar, molasses and mustard; heat until sugar is dissolved. In a large shallow casserole dish, combine beans and onion mixture. Place meatball mixture on top. Cover and bake for 1 hour or until bubbling all over.

Serves 10 to 12

African Bobotie

Meat pie African style. Serve with a crisp salad and mango chutney on the side.

1	tablespoon olive oil	15	mL
2-3	onions, chopped	2-3	
1	large clove garlic, minced	1	
2-3	tablespoons curry	25-50	mL
1	cup bread crumbs	250	mL
½	cup unsalted peanuts	125	mL
½	cup dark seedless raisins	125	mL
¾	cup chunky mango chutney	175	mL
	Juice of ½ lemon		
1	teaspoon salt	5	mL
	Freshly ground black pepper		
2	eggs	2	
2	pounds lean ground beef	1	kg
6	bay leaves	6	

Custard topping
1½	cups milk	375	mL
2	eggs	2	
½	teaspoon salt	2	mL
	Pinch of pepper		

Preheat oven to 350° F (180° C). Grease a large casserole dish (10 cup/ 2.5 L). Heat oil in a heavy skillet; sauté onions until golden. Add garlic and curry; sauté gently for 1 minute. In a separate bowl, combine bread crumbs, peanuts, raisins, chutney, lemon juice, salt, pepper and onion mixture. Lightly stir 2 eggs in a cup; add egg and meat to mixture. Combine well. Turn into casserole; top with bay leaves. Bake for 25 minutes. Remove from oven and discard bay leaves. In a separate bowl, beat remaining eggs and milk. Add salt and pepper. Pour over meat; return casserole to oven and bake for 35 minutes or until custard is set.

Serves 8

Pesto Meat Loaf

Great for brunch, lunch, dinner, picnics and ski lunches. Make ahead and serve hot or cold.

8	slices bacon, cooked crisp and crumbled (optional)	8	
½	pound lean ground beef	250	g
½	pound lean ground pork	250	g
1	spicy uncooked sausage, casing removed	1	
1	onion, finely chopped	1	
½	pound mushrooms, finely chopped	250	g
	Salt and pepper to taste		
1	egg, beaten	1	
½	cup seasoned bread crumbs	125	mL
½	cup pesto (see note below)	125	mL

Preheat oven to 375° F (190° C). In a large bowl, thoroughly mix all ingredients together. Form meat mixture into a cylindrical shape; place in a shallow roasting pan. Bake for 1¼ hours.

Serves 10 to 12

* For pesto, you can combine the following in a food processor: ½ cup (125 mL) fresh basil, ¼ cup (50 mL) grated Parmesan cheese, 2 tablespoons (25 mL) olive oil and 1 clove garlic.

* This meat loaf may also be baked encased in a pastry. Use directions from any Beef Wellington recipe and enjoy an elegant meal.

Chicken with Sausages and Peppers

Hearty country flavors.

4	fresh Italian sausages (sweet, hot or combination)	4	
2	half chicken breasts, boned and skinned	2	
2	tablespoons olive oil	25	mL
3	garlic cloves, minced	3	
2	onions, coarsely chopped	2	
1	red bell pepper, cut in 1" (2.5 cm) squares	1	
1	yellow bell pepper, cut in 1" (2.5 cm) squares	1	
1	can (28 oz/796 mL) plum tomatoes, drained	1	
½	cup chopped fresh basil (or 2 tablespoons/25 mL dried) Freshly ground pepper	125	mL

Preheat oven to 350° F (180° C). Pierce sausages several times with a fork; bake for approximately 30 minutes or until done. Drain well and cut into diagonal slices. Set aside. Cut chicken into 1" x 3" (2.5 cm x 8 cm) pieces. Heat oil in a large skillet; sauté chicken pieces just until cooked. Remove to a warm casserole. Sauté garlic and onions in oil remaining in skillet for 2 to 3 minutes. Add peppers and continue to sauté until tender-crisp. Add tomatoes, breaking apart with a fork. Add basil and pepper; simmer for 5 to 10 minutes. Return chicken and sausages to pan; heat through.

Serves 6

* To serve with pasta, do not drain tomatoes. Boil 1 cup (250 mL) chunky pasta (penne, rigatoni, fusilli etc.) until al dente; drain and add with the chicken and sausages.

Fajitas

A Mexican favorite. Great for a family; expands for a crowd. Can be made early in the day and briefly reheated at serving time.

2	pounds boneless chicken	1	kg
¼	cup fresh lime juice	50	mL
2	tablespoons tequila (optional)	25	mL
2	cloves garlic, minced	2	
1	tablespoon cumin	15	mL
1	tablespoon olive or vegetable oil	15	mL
2	cloves garlic, minced	2	
1	large Spanish onion, thinly sliced	1	
2	bell peppers (any color), julienne	2	
12	flour tortillas	12	
	Salsa		
	Guacamole (see note)		
	Sour cream (regular or light)		

Cut chicken into ¾" x 2" (2 cm x 5 cm) pieces. Place in a plastic bag or glass bowl. Combine the lime juice, tequila (if using), garlic and cumin; pour over chicken. Let marinate for 1 to 2 hours at room temperature or longer in the refrigerator. Close to serving time, heat oil in a large skillet. Drain chicken; sauté quickly, just until cooked. Remove from pan. Add garlic and onion to pan; sauté for a few minutes. Add peppers; sauté until peppers are tender-crisp. Return chicken to pan to reheat briefly. Warm tortillas in a microwave or oven; place in a covered casserole or cover with a damp cloth to keep them from drying out. To serve, spoon a quantity of chicken-pepper mixture down the center of a tortilla and garnish as desired with condiments. Fold bottom of tortilla up and then fold sides in to enclose filling. Eat from your hand.

Serves 6

* Use this same basic recipe with beef, shrimp or pork.

* Spice it way up by using hot salsa and sliced jalapeños or keep it mild by using mild salsa – your choice.

* Guacamole

2	ripe avocados	2	
1	large tomato, seeded and chopped	1	
¼	cup chopped Spanish onion	50	mL
1	large clove garlic, minced	1	
1	teaspoon ground cumin	5	mL
1-2	tablespoons fresh lime juice	15-25	mL

Peel, seed and roughly mash avocados with a fork. Stir in remaining ingredients; serve. (If guacamole must sit a while before serving, submerge an avocado pit in the dip, cover well and refrigerate.)

Honey Orange Chicken

1	cup fine dry bread crumbs	250	mL
1	tablespoon grated orange rind	15	mL
½	teaspoon salt	2	mL
¼	teaspoon pepper	1	mL
6-8	half chicken breasts, skinned and boned	6-8	
½	cup orange juice	125	mL
2-3	tablespoons butter	25-50	mL
1	chicken bouillon cube	1	
½	cup boiling water	125	mL
¼	cup butter	50	mL
½	cup honey	125	mL

Preheat oven to 350° F (180° C). In a shallow dish, combine bread crumbs, orange rind, salt and pepper. Dip each chicken breast in orange juice; then coat with crumb mixture. Melt the 2-3 tablespoons (25-50 mL) butter in a large skillet; brown chicken pieces on each side. Arrange in a single layer in a baking dish. Dissolve bouillon cube in boiling water; add the ¼ cup (50 mL) butter and honey, stirring until the butter melts. Pour over chicken; bake, basting occasionally, for about 25 minutes.

Serves 6 to 8

Sante Fe Strata

A delicious use for leftover chicken.

2	cups light sour cream	500	mL
⅓	cup milk	75	mL
1	can (28 oz/796 mL) Italian tomatoes, drained	1	
2	cloves garlic, minced	2	
¼	cup minced fresh cilantro or parsley	50	mL
1	tablespoon vegetable oil	25	mL
1	large onion, chopped	1	
2	cans (each 4 oz/110 g) diced green chilies, drained	2	
12	tortillas (each 6"/15 cm), cut in quarters	12	
2½	cups shredded cooked chicken	625	mL
2	cups shredded Monterey Jack cheese	500	mL

Preheat oven to 350° F (180° C). Mix sour cream and milk together; set aside. In a food processor or by hand, coarsely chop tomatoes, garlic and cilantro. In a fry pan, heat oil; sauté onion and chilies until onion is transparent. Combine this mixture with tomato mixture; set aside. Warm tortillas for a few seconds in the microwave oven. Spread ½ of the tortillas on the bottom of a greased 3 quart (3 L) casserole. Layer ½ of the chicken, ⅓ of the tomato sauce, ⅓ of the sour cream and ⅓ of the cheese. Repeat layers once. Layer remaining tomato sauce, sour cream and cheese on top. Bake for 40 minutes or until brown and bubbly.

Serves 6

Mussels in White Wine and Herbs

Serve with good crusty bread to help you get all of the sauce!

2-3	pounds fresh mussels	1-1.5	kg
1	tablespoon butter	15	mL
2	tablespoons olive oil	25	mL
4	shallots or green onions, chopped	4	
1	clove garlic, minced	1	
¾	cup white wine	175	mL
⅓	cup water	75	mL
3	tablespoons finely chopped fresh parsley	50	mL
	Pinch of thyme		
1-2	bay leaves	1-2	
	Freshly ground black pepper to taste		
¼	cup whipping cream	50	mL
	Extra parsley and lemon wedges for garnish		

Wash mussels under cold running water to remove all traces of dirt, seaweed and barnacles. Remove beards. Discard any broken mussels. Tap any open mussels; if they do not close, discard them. Prepare mussels just before cooking.

In a large fry pan with a cover, heat oil and butter over medium-high heat. Sauté shallots and garlic until transparent. Add wine, water, parsley, thyme, bay leaves, pepper and mussels. Pour cream over top. Cover and bring to a boil. Cook, shaking pan occasionally, for about 4 minutes or until shells open. Discard any mussels that do not open. Serve immediately in deep bowls garnished with parsley and lemon wedges.

Serves 4

* For a lighter presentation, omit the cream and substitute 2 ripe tomatoes (peeled, seeded and chopped).

Salmon Coulibiac

This Russian pie makes an elegant luncheon dish with lots of flavor.

	Pastry for 9" (23 cm) double-crust pie		
1	can (7½ oz/213 g) red sockeye salmon (undrained), flaked	1	
	Pinch of saffron		
¼	cup long-grain rice	50	mL
1	cup chopped Spanish onion	250	mL
2	tablespoons butter	25	mL
1	tablespoon vegetable oil	15	mL
1	cup sliced mushrooms	250	mL
1	tablespoon fresh lemon juice	15	mL
2	hard-boiled eggs, shelled and sliced	2	
3	tablespoons chopped fresh dill	50	mL

White Sauce

1	tablespoon butter	15	mL
1	tablespoon all-purpose flour	15	mL
1⅓	cup 10% cream or milk and cream mixed	325	mL
	Pinch of salt		
	Pinch of dry mustard		
1	teaspoon cumin	5	mL
	Pinch of pepper		

Drain juice from salmon into a ½ cup (125 mL) measure. Fill up with water. Add saffron. Use this water to cook rice. When cooked, set aside. Sauté onion in butter until transparent. Remove from pan and set aside. Add oil to pan and heat. Add mushrooms; sprinkle with lemon juice to keep them white. Sauté until all liquid evaporates. Set aside. Make white sauce by melting butter in a small saucepan over medium heat. Stir in flour and cook for 2 to 3 minutes. Add cream all at once, whisking constantly. Cook, stirring occasionally, until thickened. Season with salt, dry mustard, cumin and pepper. Set aside.

Preheat oven to 450° F (230° C). To assemble, line a 9" (23 cm) pie plate with pastry. Starting with ½ of the rice on the bottom, layer ingredients in the following order: mushrooms, ½ onions, ⅓ white sauce, one sliced egg, flaked salmon, ½ dill, ⅓ white sauce, remaining sliced egg, ½ onions, remainder of rice, remaining dill and remaining white sauce. If pie looks dry, add a little cream. Place top crust on pie. Seal and crimp edges. To allow steam to escape, prick in several places. Bake for 10 minutes; lower temperature to 375° F (190° C) for approximately 45 to 60 minutes or until pastry is brown and filling is bubbling. Let stand for 5 minutes before serving.

Serves 6

* Nice to serve with dilled hollandaise sauce or a lighter dilled yogurt sauce.

Monkfish Ragout

1	pound Italian sausage (mild or hot)	500	g
2	large onions, thinly sliced	2	
1	pound monkfish fillets, cut in 1" (2.5 cm) chunks	500	g
1	can (19 oz/540 mL) navy or white kidney beans (undrained)	1	
1	can (28 oz/796 mL) plum tomatoes (undrained)	1	
½	cup rice	125	mL
1	teaspoon dried tarragon	5	mL
2	teaspoons dried oregano	10	mL
1	bay leaf	1	
3	cloves garlic, minced	3	
	A few drops of hot pepper sauce		
	Freshly ground black pepper		
2	green bell peppers, julienne	2	
2	red bell peppers, julienne	2	
	Chopped almonds (optional)		

Pierce sausages with a fork; place in a saucepan. Cover with water and simmer for 15 minutes. Drain and slice diagonally. In a large saucepan or Dutch oven, combine all ingredients except the red and green peppers and almonds. Stir gently to combine. Cover and simmer for 30 to 40 minutes, adding peppers for the last 20 minutes. Remove bay leaf. Serve in soup bowls. Top with a sprinkle of chopped almonds (if using).

Serves 6 to 8

Smoked Salmon Pizza
and Other Embellishments
Treat food!

Crust

2	cups all-purpose flour	500	mL
1	teaspoon salt	5	mL
1	teaspoon granulated sugar	5	mL
2	teaspoons fast-rising yeast	10	mL
1	tablespoon olive or vegetable oil	15	mL
¾	cup warm water	175	mL

Topping

1	large tomato, chopped	1	
1-2	cloves garlic, minced	1-2	
6-8	green onions, chopped	6-8	
	Freshly ground pepper		
2	tablespoons chopped fresh dill	25	mL
2	cups grated Asiago cheese	500	mL
4	ounces smoked salmon, cut into bite-sized pieces	125	g
1	tablespoon capers (drained)	15	mL

To prepare dough, mix 1 cup (250 mL) of the flour, salt, sugar and yeast in a large bowl. Pour oil into water; add to yeast mixture. Mix thoroughly. Add remaining flour; knead for 3 to 5 minutes on a floured surface. Put in a greased bowl, cover and place in a warm spot for 40 minutes or until needed.

Dough can be made in the morning and kept in the refrigerator. Let it warm up for about 1 hour before using. The dough is very forgiving. Stretch dough out on an ungreased medium pizza pan or cookie sheet just before you are ready to assemble the pizza.

Preheat oven to 475° F (240° C). In a small bowl, mix tomato, garlic, green onions, pepper and dill. Spread this mixture directly on pizza crust. Sprinkle Asiago cheese on top. Bake for 10 to12 minutes on lower rack of oven. Remove from oven. Spread salmon and capers on top; return to oven for 3 minutes.

Makes an 8-slice pizza

Variations:

* Substitute red onions for the green ones and ripe olives for capers.

* Try a combination of tomato, red onion, fresh basil and oregano. Top with goat cheese and black olives.

* The tomato, onion, basil and oregano base can be used with low-fat mozzarella, chunk water-packed tuna, fresh or bottled roasted red peppers, black olives and capers. The possibilities are endless!

Fisherman's Pie
Gooood East-coast family supper.

1½	pounds cod or smoked haddock or a combination	750	g
½	cup butter	125	mL
2	cups milk	500	mL
2	bay leaves	2	
8	ounces shrimps, peeled	250	g
8	small to medium scallops	8	
3	tablespoons chopped fresh parsley	50	mL
1-2	tablespoons lemon juice	15-25	mL
2	hard-boiled eggs, coarsely chopped	2	
⅓	cup all-purpose flour	75	mL
	Salt and pepper to taste		

Topping
5-6	potatoes, freshly cooked	5-6	
2	tablespoons butter	25	mL
¼	cup sour cream	50	mL
	Nutmeg to taste		

Preheat oven to 400° F (200° C). Arrange fish in a shallow baking dish. Dot with 2 tablespoons (25 mL) of the butter; cover with milk. Add bay leaves. Bake for 20 minutes. Drain and reserve milk for use in sauce. Remove bay leaves. Remove skin and bones of fish; flake into fairly large pieces. Return to baking dish. Add shrimps, scallops, parsley, lemon juice and hard-boiled eggs. To make sauce, melt remaining butter in saucepan. Stir in flour to make a roux; cook slowly for a few minutes. Add reserved milk, stirring constantly to prevent lumps. Season with salt and pepper. Cook over low heat until thickened and smooth. Pour over seafood mixture and mix together gently.

For topping, mash potatoes with butter, sour cream and nutmeg. Spread evenly over fish mixture. (Spreads easily if fish mixture has cooled a bit.) Run the tines of a fork across the potatoes to make the surface rough. This will give a crispier result. Bake for 25 minutes until heated through and browned.

Serves 4 to 6

Pasta

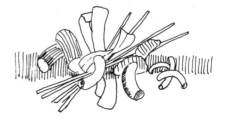

Asiago Pasta Salad

Italian cheese makes it!

Dressing

¾	cup mayonnaise	175	mL
1	large clove garlic, minced	1	
4	teaspoons finely chopped onion	20	mL
2	tablespoons balsamic vinegar	25	mL
2	tablespoons chopped fresh basil	25	mL
½	cup Asiago cheese, crumbled	125	mL

Salad

3	cups uncooked chunky pasta (rotini, radiatori or cheese tortellini)	750	mL
1	tablespoon olive oil	15	mL
½	pound asparagus, diagonally sliced, tips separated	250	g
1	sweet red pepper, coarsely diced	1	
1	sweet yellow pepper, coarsely diced	1	
6	cherry tomatoes, quartered	6	
½	cup coarsely chopped fresh parsley	125	mL

To make dressing, stir together mayonnaise, garlic, onion, vinegar, basil and ¼ cup (50 mL) of the Asiago.

Cook pasta until al dente in boiling, salted water to which the olive oil has been added. Drain well; set aside to cool, stirring occasionally. Blanch asparagus stems in boiling water for 1 minute and tips for 30 seconds. Rinse under cold water; drain well. Gently mix pasta with asparagus, peppers, tomatoes and parsley. Fold in enough dressing to moisten. Chill for several hours to blend flavors. At serving time, add more dressing if necessary. Garnish with remaining crumbled cheese.

Serves 6

* Substitute broccoli for asparagus and feta cheese for Asiago.

Orzo Artichoke Salad

Make this a day ahead, then sit back and relax.

1½	cups orzo (rice-shaped pasta)	375	mL
¼	cup olive oil	50	mL
1	can (14 oz/398 mL) artichoke hearts, drained and diced	1	
4	ounces prosciutto ham, diced	125	g
4	green onions, chopped	4	
½	cup chopped fresh parsley	125	mL
½	cup grated Parmesan cheese	125	mL
	Parsley or fresh basil for garnish		

Dressing

1	egg yolk	1	
	Salt and pepper to taste		
2	tablespoons white wine vinegar	25	mL
2	tablespoons fresh lemon juice	25	mL
1	teaspoon Dijon mustard	5	mL
½	cup olive oil	125	mL

Cook pasta in lots of boiling, salted water until al dente. Rinse under cold water and drain. In large bowl, toss with the ¼ cup (50 mL) oil. Add artichoke hearts, prosciutto, green onions, parsley and Parmesan. Toss well.

To make dressing, combine egg yolk, salt, pepper, vinegar, lemon juice and mustard in a blender or food processor. Add the ½ cup (125 mL) oil in a thin stream while machine is running. Blend until thick. Toss with pasta mixture; chill. Transfer to a serving bowl and garnish lavishly with parsley.

Serves 8

Spicy Sesame Noodles
Serve alone or with cold meat – delicious.

1	pound linguine or spaghetti	500	g
2	tablespoons sesame oil	25	mL
¼	cup sesame paste (tahini) or creamy peanut butter	50	mL
¼	cup soy sauce	50	mL
2	tablespoons wine vinegar	25	mL
2	tablespoons grated fresh ginger	25	mL
¼	teaspoon crushed red pepper flakes	1	mL
2-3	red bell peppers, roasted and cut into slivers	2-3	
4	scallions, cut into slivers	4	

Cook pasta in boiling, salted water until al dente. Drain, toss with sesame oil and set aside. In a bowl, combine sesame paste, soy sauce, wine vinegar, ginger and red pepper flakes; toss with noodles. Gently toss in roasted red peppers and scallions. Serve at room temperature.

Serves 4 as a main course, 6 as an appetizer

* To roast red peppers, place under the broiler or on the barbecue. Turn frequently until black all over. Place in a paper or plastic bag and allow to steam until cool enough to handle. Peel, remove seeds and slice.

* Make an even more colorful dish by adding steamed, sliced snow peas.

Tortellini Roquefort Salad
For blue-cheese aficionados!

½	pound cheese tortellini	250	g
1	tablespoon olive oil	15	mL
1	sweet red pepper, julienne	1	
1	sweet yellow pepper, julienne	1	
1	small head broccoli (tips only), cut into small florets	1	
4	green onions, diagonally sliced	4	
1	cup chopped fresh parsley	250	mL
	Freshly ground black pepper		
¼	pound Roquefort cheese, crumbled	125	g

Dressing

¼	cup grainy Dijon mustard	50	mL
1¾	cups mayonnaise	425	mL

Cook tortellini in boiling, salted water until al dente. Drain well; toss with olive oil. When cool, toss with peppers, broccoli, green onions, parsley, black pepper and Roquefort. Whisk mustard and mayonnaise together in a small bowl. Toss with the tortellini mixture; chill until serving time.

Serves 6 to 8

Seafood Pasta Salad with Basil Cream
Wonderful make-ahead salad.

½	pound rotini or fettuccine, broken	250	g
¼	cup light olive oil	50	mL
2	tablespoons white wine vinegar	25	mL
1	teaspoon red wine vinegar	5	mL
	Salt and pepper to taste		
8	thin asparagus spears, cut in 1½" (4 cm) pieces	8	
1¼	cups broccoli florets	300	mL
3	scallions, minced	3	
1	cup cherry tomatoes	250	mL
1¼	cups tiny peas (fresh or frozen) or snow peas (blanched and halved)	300	mL
1	pound bay scallops	500	g
1	pound large shrimps, cooked, shelled, and deveined	500	g

Marinade for Seafood

¼	cup olive oil	50	mL
1	tablespoon white wine vinegar	15	mL
1	tablespoon red wine vinegar	15	mL
1	small clove garlic, minced	1	
1	scallion, minced	1	
	Salt and pepper to taste		

Dressing

¼	cup white wine vinegar	50	mL
1	tablespoon Dijon mustard	15	mL
¼	cup tightly packed fresh basil (or 1-3 tablespoons/15-50 mL dried)	50	mL
1	clove garlic	1	
¼	cup vegetable oil	50	mL
2	tablespoons chopped fresh parsley	25	mL
¼	cup whipping cream	50	mL
½	cup sour cream	125	mL

The pasta, vegetables and dressing can be prepared 1 to 2 days ahead and kept in the refrigerator. The seafood should be prepared the day of serving.

Cook pasta in boiling, salted water until al dente. Drain. Toss with oil, vinegars, salt and pepper. Refrigerate. Cook asparagus and broccoli until tender-crisp. Drain and cool in running cold water; drain again. Combine scallions with tomatoes. Steam fresh peas slightly or use defrosted, uncooked frozen peas. Store each vegetable in separate containers in refrigerator. Several hours before serving, rinse scallops. Place in saucepan and add water to just cover. Bring to a boil and simmer for a few minutes until opaque and tender; drain. Combine marinade ingredients; toss with scallops and shrimps. Refrigerate. For dressing, combine vinegar, mustard, basil and garlic in food processor or blender. Mix until almost smooth. Add oil gradually, then parsley, whipping cream and sour cream. Blend until smooth. Refrigerate.

Thirty minutes before serving, stir dressing. Combine pasta, vegetables, seafood and dressing; toss until coated.

Serves 6 generously

* Chicken may be substituted for the seafood. Use 6 half breasts of chicken (skinned, boned and cooked). Cut in bite-sized pieces.

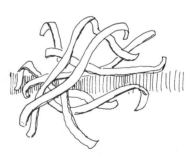

Spinach Lasagne with Sunflower Seeds

¾	pound lasagne noodles	375	g
1	package (10 oz/284 g) fresh spinach	1	
3	cups tomato sauce (recipe follows) or use your own favorite	750	mL
½	cup sunflower seeds, toasted	125	mL
¾	cup ricotta cheese, mixed with enough milk to make spreadable	175	mL
½	cup grated Parmesan cheese	125	mL
1	pound mozzarella cheese, shredded	500	g

Preheat oven to 350° F (180° C). Cook noodles in boiling, salted water until al dente; drain, rinse and set aside. Wash spinach and tear into bite-sized pieces. With just the water clinging to the leaves, cook briefly. Drain and squeeze dry. Spread ¾ cup (175 mL) of the tomato sauce in the bottom of a 13" x 9" (3.5 L) lasagne pan. Place ⅓ of the noodles on top. Cover with ½ of the spinach, ⅓ of the seeds, ½ of the ricotta, ⅓ of the Parmesan, ⅓ of the mozzarella. Repeat these layers once. For the final layer, use ¾ cup (175 mL) sauce, remaining noodles, seeds, Parmesan and mozzarella. Top with the remaining sauce. Don't be afraid to press down gently if dish seems too full. Lasagne may be refrigerated several hours before baking. Bring to room temperature. Bake for 40 minutes and let stand for 10 minutes before serving.

Serves 6 to 8

* Try grating a little nutmeg over the spinach while assembling the lasagne.

Tomato Sauce

½	cup vegetable oil	125	mL
1	large onion, finely chopped	1	
2	cloves garlic, minced	2	
2	cans (each 28 oz/796 mL) plum tomatoes	2	
4	teaspoons dried basil (or ¼ cup/50 mL chopped fresh)	20	mL
	Salt and pepper to taste		

Heat ¼ cup (50 mL) of the oil in a heavy pan. Sauté onion and garlic over medium heat until transparent. Add tomatoes, breaking apart with a wooden spoon. Add basil, salt and pepper; cook over medium heat, stirring occasionally, for 20 minutes. Add remaining oil; stir.

Pasta Salad with Smoked Salmon

1	package (12 oz/340 g) 3-color pasta spirals	1	
1	cup sour cream	250	mL
⅓	cup mayonnaise	75	mL
2	tablespoons balsamic vinegar	25	mL
	Chopped fresh chives or green onions to taste		
	Chopped fresh dill to taste		
1	cup frozen green peas	250	mL
½	pound smoked salmon, cut in strips	250	g
	Dill for garnish		

Cook pasta according to package instructions. Rinse in cold water and let cool. Mix sour cream and mayonnaise. Add balsamic vinegar. Mix well. Add chives and dill. Mix sour cream mixture with pasta; add frozen peas. Refrigerate. Just before serving, add smoked salmon strips. Garnish with dill.

Serves 4 to 6

Orzo Parmesan Gratin

Delicious substitute for potatoes, rice or other pasta.

1	pound orzo (rice-shaped pasta), about 3 cups (750 mL)	500	g
6	cloves garlic, unpeeled	6	
1	cup whipping cream	250	mL
1	cup chicken broth	250	mL
1	cup freshly grated Parmesan cheese	250	mL
1	cup minced fresh parsley	250	mL
¼	cup bread crumbs	50	mL
2	tablespoons (approx.) unsalted butter, melted	25	mL

Preheat oven to 325° F (160° C). Cook orzo in boiling, salted water with garlic cloves for 8 to 10 minutes or until al dente. Drain in a colander and rinse well with cold water. Drain again. Remove the garlic cloves; peel and mash garlic with a fork. In a large bowl, whisk mashed garlic with cream. Add orzo, broth, ¾ cup (175 mL) of the Parmesan and ¾ cup (175 mL) of the parsley. Combine mixture well. Transfer to a buttered, shallow, 2-quart (2 L) baking dish; smooth the top. In a small bowl, toss bread crumbs, butter, remaining Parmesan and remaining parsley; sprinkle evenly over the orzo mixture. Bake for 1 hour and 15 minutes or until bubbly around the edge and golden brown.

Serves 8 to 10

* This recipe may easily be halved. Reduce the cooking time to 40 minutes.

Rotini with Broccoli and Chèvre

1	pound rotini or other chunky pasta	500	g
¾	cup unsalted butter, cut in pieces	175	mL
6	cups packed broccoli florets, blanched for 30 seconds	1.5	L
1	pound creamy chèvre, cut in pieces	500	g
	Salt and freshly ground pepper		

Cook pasta in a large pot of boiling, salted water until al dente. Drain. In the meantime, melt butter over moderate heat in a large fry pan. Add broccoli; toss until well coated, about 2 minutes. Add chèvre; stir until it melts and coats the broccoli. Pour over hot pasta. Season with salt and pepper to taste. Serve immediately.

Serves 4 to 6

Fettuccini alla Palermo

A treat for smoked salmon fans.

2	tablespoons butter	25	mL
2	shallots, finely chopped	2	
1	clove garlic, minced	1	
1	cup vodka	250	mL
1	cup whipping cream	250	mL
8	ounces smoked salmon	250	g
	Salt and freshly ground pepper to taste		
8	ounces fettuccini	250	g
2	tablespoons butter	25	mL
	Freshly grated Parmesan cheese		

In a medium saucepan, melt butter and sauté shallots until transparent. Add garlic and sauté an additional 2 minutes. Add vodka and simmer until liquid is reduced by half. Add cream and simmer until desired thickness. Stir in salmon and cook just until heated through. Season with salt and pepper. Meanwhile, cook fettuccini in a large pot of boiling water until al dente. Drain, transfer to a warm serving dish and toss with butter. Toss again with sauce. Serve immediately with Parmesan cheese.

Serves 4

Fresh Tomato Pasta

Best when tomatoes are in season.

⅓	cup extra virgin olive oil	75	mL
3	cloves garlic, minced	3	
3	large tomatoes, peeled, seeded and diced	3	
⅔	cup diced red onion	150	mL
1	ripe avocado, diced and tossed with	1	
2	tablespoons lime juice	25	mL
⅓	cup drained capers	75	mL
½	cup chopped fresh parsley	125	mL
	Salt and freshly ground pepper to taste		
½	pound spaghetti	250	g

In large bowl, combine all ingredients except spaghetti. Stir and let marinate for at least 30 minutes. Cook spaghetti in boiling, salted water until al dente. Drain well and immediately toss with the sauce.

Serves 4

* Replace capers with 2 teaspoons (10 mL) ground cumin and 1 can (4 oz/110 g) green chilies, drained and chopped.

Eggplant Rotini
Healthy and economical.

1	large eggplant	1	
3	tablespoons sunflower oil	50	mL
4	large cloves garlic, minced	4	
2	large onions, coarsely chopped	2	
1	can (28 oz/796 mL) tomatoes	1	
¾	cup chopped fresh basil	175	mL
¼	cup chopped fresh parsley	50	mL
1	teaspoon salt	5	mL
	Freshly ground pepper		
1	package (2 lb/900 g) rotini	1	
	Grated Parmesan cheese		

Cut unpeeled eggplant into 1" (2.5 cm) cubes. Soak eggplant in cold, salted water for 30 minutes. Drain; pat dry. Heat oil in large skillet. Sauté garlic, onions, and eggplant for 10 minutes. Add tomatoes, basil, parsley, salt and pepper. Simmer for about 30 minutes. Just before serving, cook rotini in a large pot of boiling, salted water. Drain; toss with hot sauce. Serve immediately with Parmesan cheese.

Serves 4 to 6

* To add meat to the meal, add sliced, cooked Italian sausage.

Tomato and Garlic Penne

A versatile sauce that's even better when made with fresh tomatoes.

3	tablespoons olive oil	50	mL
1	cup finely chopped onion	250	mL
1	tablespoon finely chopped garlic	15	mL
2	cans (each 19 oz/540 mL) tomatoes, chopped	2	
1	can (5½ oz/156 mL) tomato paste	1	
2-3	teaspoons dried oregano, crumbled	10-15	mL
1	teaspoon dried basil, crumbled	5	mL
1	bay leaf	1	
1-2	tablespoons granulated sugar	15-25	mL
½	teaspoon salt	2	mL
	Black pepper to taste		
5	cups penne (uncooked)	1.25	L
	Parmesan cheese (freshly grated, if possible)		

Heat olive oil in a large saucepan over moderate heat. Sauté onion and garlic for 5 to 7 minutes until soft but not brown. Stir in remaining ingredients except penne and Parmesan; bring to a boil. Reduce heat to very low; simmer, uncovered, stirring occasionally, for about 1 hour. Remove bay leaf. Just before serving, cook penne in a large pot of boiling, salted water until al dente. Drain; toss with hot sauce. Serve immediately with Parmesan cheese.

Serves 4 to 6

* The sauce makes about 3 cups (750 mL) and freezes well.

* The sauce is outstanding when made with fresh tomatoes. Substitute 4 cups (1 L) chopped fresh tomatoes for canned.

* Try drained clams, cooked shrimp or cooked scallops mixed with the sauce and served over the pasta of your choice. Thin sauce with a little clam juice, tomato juice or whipping cream. (A lighter cream will curdle.)

Spinach Roll-ups
A tasty main course or appetizer.

1	tablespoon vegetable oil	15	mL
3	leeks (white part only), chopped	3	
3	green onions, finely chopped	3	
1	clove garlic, minced	1	
1	cup chopped mushrooms	250	mL
1	small sweet red pepper, chopped	1	
1½	pounds fresh spinach, washed and dried	750	g
1	tablespoon dried basil	15	mL
1	teaspoon dried oregano	5	mL
¼	cup bread crumbs	50	mL
	Pinch of nutmeg		
3	tablespoons grated Parmesan cheese	50	mL
½	cup grated mozzarella cheese	125	mL
1	egg, lightly beaten	1	
1	cup ricotta cheese	250	mL
8-10	lasagna noodles (half green, half white)	8-10	
2	cups tomato sauce	500	mL

Topping
1	cup shredded mozzarella cheese	250	mL
2	tablespoons grated Parmesan cheese	25	mL
	Fresh parsley for garnish		

Heat oil in a large fry pan over medium heat. Sauté leeks, green onions and garlic until golden. Add mushrooms; sauté until just cooked. Add red pepper; sauté for a few minutes. Coarsely chop spinach; add to the pan and cook until limp. Add herbs, bread crumbs, nutmeg, the 3 tablespoons (50 mL) Parmesan and the ½ cup (125 mL) mozzarella. Mix well. Set aside to cool. Mix egg and ricotta together; add to spinach mixture. Refrigerate. (Tastes best if made a day ahead.)

Cook lasagna noodles according to package directions. Drain; pat dry. Pour a thin layer of tomato sauce in a 13" x 9" (3.5 L) baking dish. Spread 2 to 3 tablespoons (25-50 mL) of the spinach mixture over each noodle, covering entirely. Roll noodle up loosely, end to end. Place spinach rolls in the dish. Pour remaining sauce over the rolls. Sprinkle with the topping cheeses. Cover and refrigerate until needed.

Preheat oven to 350° F (180° C). Bake, uncovered, for 35 to 40 minutes or until bubbly. To serve, lift rolls onto plates and garnish with a sprig of parsley. Rolls may also be cut in half horizontally and stood on end.

Serves 4 as a main course, 8 as an appetizer

Tomato-Bacon Linguine
Simple and flavorful.

½	pound bacon	250	g
2	large onions, chopped	2	
3	cloves garlic, minced	3	
2	cans (each 28 oz/796 mL) plum tomatoes	2	
1½	teaspoons granulated sugar	7	mL
1	teaspoon dried tarragon	5	mL
½	teaspoon freshly ground black pepper	2	mL
¼	teaspoon salt	1	mL
¼	teaspoon cayenne	1	mL
2	pounds linguine	1	kg
¼	cup finely chopped fresh parsley	50	mL
	Parmesan cheese (freshly grated if possible)		

In a large fry pan, cook bacon until crisp; drain, crumble coarsely and reserve. Remove all but ¼ cup (50 mL) of fat from pan. Add onions; cook for 5 minutes over medium heat or until golden. Stir in garlic, tomatoes, sugar, tarragon, pepper, salt and cayenne. Cover and simmer gently for 20 to 25 minutes, stirring occasionally. Cook pasta according to package directions in a large pot of boiling, salted water; drain. Meanwhile, stir bacon and parsley into sauce; simmer, uncovered, for 5 minutes to thicken slightly. Toss pasta with sauce. Sprinkle with Parmesan.

Serves 8

Dilled Seafood Gratin with Orzo and Artichokes

1	can (14 oz/398 mL) artichoke hearts	1	
1	can (7 oz/198 g) solid white tuna	1	
1	cup cooked orzo (rice-shaped pasta)	250	mL
½	pound raw shrimps, peeled and deveined	250	g
2	tablespoons vegetable oil	25	mL
½	pound mushrooms, thinly sliced	250	g
2	cloves garlic, minced	2	
1	cup thinly sliced green onions	250	mL
3	tablespoons butter	50	mL
¼	cup all-purpose flour	50	mL
2	cups chicken broth	500	mL
3	tablespoons fresh lemon juice	50	mL
¾	cup grated Parmesan cheese	175	mL
2	tablespoons snipped fresh dill	25	mL
	Salt and pepper to taste		
½	cup bread crumbs	125	mL

Preheat oven to 400° F (200° C). Drain artichoke hearts; cut into bite-sized pieces. Drain and flake tuna. Place orzo, artichokes and tuna in a 1½-quart (1.5 L) gratin dish. Add shrimp. Heat oil in a fry pan over medium heat; sauté mushrooms and garlic until liquid from mushrooms evaporates. Add green onions; sauté briefly. Add mushroom mixture to the artichoke mixture. In a small saucepan, melt butter over low heat. Stir in flour; cook roux for 3 minutes. Add chicken broth in a steady stream while whisking. Continue to whisk while mixture comes to a boil. Lower heat; cook for 5 minutes, stirring occasionally. Remove from heat; add lemon juice and ½ cup (125 mL) of the Parmesan cheese. Add sauce, dill, salt and pepper to artichoke mixture. Gently combine ingredients. Toss remaining Parmesan with bread crumbs; sprinkle over top. Bake for 25 to 30 minutes until topping is golden and liquid is bubbling.

Serves 4 to 6

Elegant Entrees

Grilled Chicken with Sun-Dried Tomato Vinaigrette

Perhaps the best chicken you'll ever eat! Our thanks to Chef Peter George.

4	half chicken breasts, skinned and boned	4

Marinade

2	tablespoons olive oil	25 mL
1	clove garlic, chopped	1
1	tablespoon chopped sun-dried tomatoes plus some oil from tomatoes	15 mL
1½	teaspoons lemon or orange zest	7 mL
1	tablespoon balsamic vinegar	15 mL
1	tablespoon pesto or chopped fresh basil	15 mL
1	tablespoon chopped fresh Italian parsley	15 mL

Warm Vinaigrette

1	tomato, peeled, seeded and chopped	1
1	clove garlic, chopped	1
1	teaspoon fresh basil or pesto	5 mL
2	teaspoons balsamic vinegar	10 mL
	Juice of ½ lemon	
2	tablespoons olive oil	25 mL
1½	teaspoons pine nuts	7 mL
2	tablespoons julienne sun-dried tomatoes	25 mL
1	tablespoon chopped fresh Italian parsley	15 mL

Mix marinade ingredients together; pour over chicken breasts in a plastic bag. Close bag tightly. Marinate in the refrigerator for at least 3 hours or overnight. One hour before serving time, remove chicken and marinade from refrigerator; let come to room temperature. Grill over medium heat until just done. Be careful not to overcook. To make vinaigrette, mix all vinaigrette ingredients together; warm (but do not boil). Serve with hot grilled chicken breasts. Vinaigrette will separate – stir as you serve.

Serves 4

Rolled Stuffed Chicken Breasts

Quick to prepare, impressive to serve.

4	half chicken breasts, boned and skinned	4
1	package (4 oz/125 g) cream cheese, softened	1
2-3	green onions with tops, finely sliced	2-3
	Salt and pepper to taste	
1	teaspoon Beau Monde or ground celery seed or thyme	5 mL
4	strips bacon	4
	Green onions for garnish	

Pound chicken breasts between 2 sheets of waxed paper until very thin. Add green onions, salt, pepper and Beau Monde to cream cheese. Mix until smooth. Place approximately 1 tablespoon (15 mL) of the cheese mixture in the center of each chicken breast half. Roll up, tucking sides in. Wrap with bacon; skewer with toothpicks. Broil in oven 4"-5" (10 cm-12 cm) from heat for approximately 5 to 10 minutes per side. Watch carefully and do not overcook. Serve whole or sliced, attractively arranged on a platter. Garnish with diagonally sliced green onions.

Serves 4

Crab-Stuffed Chicken Breasts

8	half chicken breasts, boned and skinned	8	
3	tablespoons butter	50	mL
¼	cup all-purpose flour	50	mL
¾	cup milk	175	mL
¾	cup chicken broth	175	mL
⅓	cup white wine	75	mL
1	tablespoon butter	15	mL
1	small onion, chopped	1	
1	cup chopped mushrooms	250	mL
2	tablespoons chopped fresh parsley	25	mL
½	cup soda cracker crumbs	125	mL
1	package (7 oz/200 g) frozen crab [or 2 cans (each 4.2 oz/120 g) crab, drained well]	1	
3	tablespoons grated Asiago or Swiss cheese	50	mL
1	teaspoon paprika	5	mL

Preheat oven to 350° F (180 °C). Pound each chicken breast to ¼" (5 mm) thickness between two sheets of waxed paper. In a large saucepan, melt the 3 tablespoons (50 mL) butter over medium heat. Stir in flour; cook briefly. Add milk, chicken broth and wine, stirring constantly. Continue stirring until thick and smooth. Melt the 1 tablespoon (15 mL) butter in a fry pan; sauté onion until transparent. Add mushrooms and parsley; cook gently for 2 to 3 minutes. Stir in cracker crumbs, crab and 2 tablespoons (25 mL) of the sauce. Place about ¼ cup (50 mL) of the crab mixture in the center of each chicken breast. Fold over and press edges together. Place in a baking pan, cover with sauce and bake for 30 to 40 minutes or until sauce is bubbly. Mix cheese and paprika together; sprinkle over chicken. Return to the oven until cheese is melted.

Serves 8

Chicken with Oranges and Snow Peas

Very light and fresh-tasting.

8	half chicken breasts, boned and skinned	8
1	can (6 oz/178 mL) frozen orange juice concentrate	1
1	package dry onion soup mix	1
2	cups water	500 mL
1	can (10 oz/284 mL) sliced water chestnuts, drained	1
1	can (10 oz/284 mL) mandarin oranges, drained	1
18	snow peas, slivered	18
	Toasted cashew nuts for garnish (optional)	

Preheat oven to 350° F (180° C). Slice chicken into 1" (2.5 cm) slices. Heat 3 tablespoons (50 mL) of the orange juice concentrate in a fry pan; add chicken. Sauté for about 5 minutes. Meanwhile, combine onion soup mix, water and remaining orange juice concentrate in a large casserole dish. Add chicken, water chestnuts and oranges. Bake, uncovered, for 20 minutes. Then add snow peas and bake for 5 minutes. Garnish with cashew nuts (if using).

Serves 6 to 8

* Substitute ¾ cup (175 mL) fresh orange sections (skin and membrane removed) for mandarin oranges.

Tarragon and Lime-Glazed Chicken

Serve hot, cold or at room temperature – you can't go wrong.

6-8	half chicken breasts, boned and skinned	6-8	
¼	cup butter	50	mL
⅓	cup honey	75	mL
¼	cup Dijon mustard	50	mL
2-3	tablespoons chopped fresh tarragon (or 1 tablespoon/15 mL dried)	25-50	mL
½	lime (juice and finely grated rind)	½	

Preheat oven to 350° F (180° C). Place chicken breasts in a shallow baking dish large enough to hold them without crowding. In a saucepan or a large measuring cup, mix remaining ingredients. Bring to a boil on the stove or in the microwave oven. Remove from heat; pour over chicken. Bake for 20 to 30 minutes, depending on the size of the breasts. Baste occasionally with the sauce to glaze. Be very careful not to overcook. Chicken is done when no longer pink and juices run clear. Serve warm or cold.

Serves 4 to 6

*Doubles or triples well to feed a crowd.

Chicken Glazed with Balsamic Vinegar and Basil

Light and refreshing – perfect for a picnic or summer eating.

6-8	half chicken breasts, boned and skinned	6-8	
¼	cup butter	50	mL
⅓	cup honey	75	mL
¼	cup Dijon mustard	50	mL
2	tablespoons balsamic vinegar	25	mL
1	clove garlic, minced	1	
2	tablespoons chopped fresh basil	25	mL
	Salt and pepper to taste		

Preheat oven to 350° F (180° C). Place chicken breasts in a shallow baking dish large enough to hold them without crowding. In a saucepan, bring remaining ingredients to a boil. Remove from heat; pour over chicken. Bake for 20 to 30 minutes, depending on the size of the chicken breasts. Baste occasionally with the sauce to glaze. Be very careful not to overcook; chicken is done when no longer pink and juices run clear. Serve warm or cold.

Serves 6 to 8

Elegant Buffet Chicken

¼	cup butter	50	mL
½	cup chopped celery	125	mL
1	clove garlic, minced	1	
¼	cup all-purpose flour	50	mL
2	cups milk	500	mL
1	can (10 oz/284 mL) mushroom soup	1	
1	package (8 oz/250 g) cream cheese, cut into chunks	1	
½	cup coarsely chopped sweet pimiento	125	mL
½	cup sliced pimiento-filled olives	125	mL
½	pound fresh mushrooms, sliced	250	g
3	tablespoons butter	50	mL
	Salt and pepper to taste		
12	half chicken breasts, skinned, boned and cut into bite-sized pieces	12	
1	cup buttered bread crumbs	250	mL

Preheat oven to 350° F (180° C). In a large saucepan, melt butter over medium heat. Add celery and garlic; sauté briefly. Add flour; cook for 2 to 3 minutes, stirring. Whisk in milk and bring to a boil. Add mushroom soup and cream cheese. Stir until smooth; bring to a boil and remove from heat. Add pimiento and olives. In a separate fry pan, sauté mushrooms in the 3 tablespoons (50 mL) butter until moisture evaporates; add to creamed mixture along with salt and pepper. Add chicken if baking immediately. (If not baking immediately, let sauce mixture cool before adding chicken.) Place in a large greased casserole dish; cover with buttered bread crumbs. Can be frozen before baking. Bake for 45 to 60 minutes.

Serves 12

Chicken Breasts with Grapefruit

4	half chicken breasts, boned and skinned	4
	Juice of 1 lime	
	Salt and pepper	
2	tablespoons all-purpose flour	25 mL
2	tablespoons unsalted butter or	25 mL
	vegetable oil	
1	tablespoon chopped shallots or onions	15 mL
2	tablespoons rum	25 mL
½	cup chicken stock	125 mL
¼	cup sherry	50 mL
	Juice of ½ grapefruit	
	Sections of ½ grapefruit, membranes removed	
	Chopped fresh chives or parsley	

Flatten the chicken breasts to ½" (1.25 cm); sprinkle with lime juice, salt and pepper. Let stand for 5 minutes. Coat chicken with flour. Heat butter in a 10" (25 cm) fry pan over medium heat. Sauté chicken breasts for approximately 5 minutes or until just done, adding shallots halfway through the cooking time. Remove chicken to a warm platter and keep hot. Drain accumulated fat from fry pan. Add rum, stock, sherry and grapefruit juice to pan. Boil sauce until reduced by half. Add grapefruit sections; heat. Adjust seasonings. Pour over hot chicken breasts. Garnish with chives.

Serves 4

Never-Fail Filet of Beef

Simple, impressive, elegant meal! Add your favorite sauce!

2	pounds filet of beef	1	kg
1	tablespoon dry mustard	15	mL
1-2	cloves garlic, minced	1-2	
2	tablespoons butter	25	mL
	Lots of freshly ground black pepper		

Dry outside of beef with paper towel. Make a paste with the mustard, garlic and butter. Rub the paste all over the meat. Sprinkle well with black pepper. Place on a rack in a shallow roasting pan. Allow meat to come to room temperature, about 1 hour. Preheat oven to 450° F (230° C). Place meat in center of oven; immediately reduce heat to 400° F (200° C). Roast meat for about 35 minutes for rare, or longer according to personal taste. Remove from oven and let stand for 10 minutes before slicing, or let cool completely and serve cold.

Serves 6

* We suggest serving this with one of the following sauces: Creamy Horseradish Sauce with Apple (see page 193); Roasted Red Pepper Sauce (see page 192); Sassy Sauce (see page 193).

Filet of Beef with Black Pepper Vinaigrette

2	pounds filet of beef, roasted	1	kg
1	bunch leeks (white part only)	1	
1	clove garlic, minced	1	
2-3	tablespoons (total) butter and olive oil mixed	25-50	mL
3	cups sliced mushrooms	750	mL
	Salt and pepper to taste		

Vinaigrette

¼	cup olive oil	50	mL
1½	teaspoons black peppercorns, coarsely cracked	7	mL
1	tablespoon red wine vinegar	15	mL
1½	teaspoons balsamic vinegar	7	mL
½	teaspoon Dijon mustard	2	mL
¼	teaspoon dried thyme	1	mL
¼	teaspoon dried oregano	1	mL
	Salt to taste		

Roast filet as directed in Never-Fail Filet of Beef (see page 100). Chop cleaned white parts of leeks in 1" (2.5 cm) half rounds. Heat butter and olive oil in fry pan with garlic. Sauté leeks and mushrooms until tender. Place on warm platter. Slice beef in thick slices; lay beef, overlapping slices, on top of vegetables. Keep warm.

To make vinaigrette, in a small round-bottomed pan, heat cracked peppercorns in oil until peppers soften slightly. Whisk in vinegars, mustard, herbs and salt. Drizzle a little of the warm vinaigrette over the meat. Pass remainder in a sauce boat. Vinaigrette can be made ahead of time and warmed at serving time.

Serves 6

* To coarsely crack black peppercorns, place in a heavy plastic bag and pound with a rolling pin or the bottom of a heavy pot.

* If available, use shiitake mushrooms.

World's Best Pepper Steak

The name says it all!

1	large flank steak (or 2 small)	1

Marinade

½	cup vegetable oil	125 mL
¼	cup soy sauce	50 mL
¼	cup lemon juice	50 mL
2	tablespoons coarsely crushed peppercorns	25 mL
2	tablespoons celery seed	25 mL
2	tablespoons finely chopped onion	25 mL
2	cloves garlic, minced	2

Place steak in a plastic bag or in a shallow glass dish. Mix the marinade ingredients together and pour over steak. Marinate in the refrigerator for 24 hours. Bring steak to room temperature. Remove from marinade; broil or barbecue for 5 to 7 minutes per side. Slice across the grain. Marinade may be heated and served as a sauce.

Serves 4 to 6

Pork Medallions in Mustard Cream

A wonderful aroma – tastes even better!

2½	pounds pork tenderloin	1.25	kg
¼	cup all-purpose flour	50	mL
½	teaspoon salt	2	mL
¼	teaspoon white pepper	1	mL
2	tablespoons olive oil	25	mL

Sauce

¼	cup butter	50	mL
1	clove garlic, minced	1	
¼	cup all-purpose flour	50	mL
¼	cup Dijon mustard	50	mL
½	cup dry white wine	125	mL
1	cup milk	250	mL
½	teaspoon salt	2	mL
½	teaspoon dried basil	2	mL
½	cup 10% cream or milk	125	mL

Preheat oven to 350° F (180° C). Cut pork into ¾" (2 cm) medallions. Pound gently to flatten. Combine flour, salt and pepper. Dredge pork in flour mixture. Heat oil in a fry pan over medium-high heat, and brown pork for 5 to 10 minutes, turning once. Arrange in a single layer in a shallow baking dish.

To make sauce, melt butter in the same fry pan over medium heat; sauté garlic briefly. Stir in flour to make a smooth paste. Add mustard; cook for 2 to 3 minutes. Whisk in wine, milk, salt and basil. Cook, whisking constantly, until bubbly and thickened. Remove from heat. Whisk in the cream. Heat sauce to just below the boiling point; pour over pork. Recipe can be prepared 1 day in advance. Cover and refrigerate. Before serving, bring pork to room temperature. Reheat, covered, in a 350° F (180° C) oven for 15 to 20 minutes or until hot.

Serves 8 to 10

* For extra zip, blanch the zest of 1 orange. Garnish with orange zest and seedless green grapes after baking.

Pork Tenderloin in Rum Marinade

Delectable!

3	pork tenderloins	3

Marinade

2	tablespoons brown sugar	25 mL
¼	cup rum	50 mL
¼	cup soy sauce	50 mL

Sauce

⅓	cup sour cream	75 mL
⅓	cup mayonnaise	75 mL
1½	teaspoons dry mustard	7 mL
2-3	green onions, finely chopped	2-3

Combine all marinade ingredients in a plastic bag or a glass container. Add tenderloins; marinate for 4 to 5 hours, turning occasionally. Combine sauce ingredients; refrigerate for several hours to allow flavors to blend.

Preheat oven to 325° F (160° C). Place a shallow pan of water on bottom rack of oven to ensure moist tenderloins. Remove tenderloins from marinade (reserve marinade) and bake in a shallow baking pan for 45 minutes to 1 hour, basting 3 to 4 times. To serve, slice in ½" (1.25 cm) slices. Bring the marinade to a boil. Offer a choice of sauce and marinade with the meat.

Serves 6 to 8

Pork Chops with Apples and Raisins

A cool-weather favorite.

½	cup seedless raisins	125	mL
1	tablespoon vegetable oil	15	mL
6	center-cut loin pork chops	6	
5	tart apples, peeled, cored and quartered	5	
12	small white onions, peeled	12	
1	tablespoon brown sugar	15	mL
1	cup beef stock	250	mL
	Salt and pepper to taste		
¼-½	teaspoon ground cloves	1-2	mL
2	sprigs thyme (or ¼ teaspoon/1 mL dried)	2	
	Pinch of nutmeg		
	Pinch of mace		
1	tablespoon red currant jelly	15	mL

Preheat oven to 350° F (180° C). Pour boiling water over raisins; let stand until plump. Meanwhile, heat oil in a fry pan over medium-high heat; brown chops for 4 to 5 minutes. Place in a casserole. Arrange apples and onions on top. Drain raisins; add to casserole; sprinkle with sugar. Add seasonings to stock; mix well. Pour over casserole; cover and bake for 1 hour. Stir in currant jelly.

Serves 6

* Try with a 4-5 lb (2-2.5 kg) pork loin roast. Bake for 2½ hours, basting frequently.

Cranberry-Prune Stuffed Pork Tenderloin

2	pork tenderloins of equal size	2
½	cup chopped onion	125 mL
½	cup pitted and chopped dried prunes	125 mL
1	cup cranberry sauce	250 mL
½	cup bread crumbs	125 mL
2	tablespoons butter or margarine, melted	25 mL
2	tablespoons chopped fresh parsley	25 mL
1¼	cups water	300 mL
2	strips bacon	2
1	tablespoon all-purpose flour	15 mL
	Parsley or mint for garnish	

Preheat oven to 325° F (160° C). Split pork tenderloins lengthwise and ⅔ through. Flatten each one slightly between sheets of waxed paper to even out thickness. In a bowl, mix onion, prunes, ¾ cup (175 mL) of the cranberry sauce, bread crumbs and butter. Combine well; toss with parsley. Place stuffing mixture lengthwise on 1 opened tenderloin; shape into an oblong. Place second tenderloin on top with the thin end of one tenderloin over the fat end of the other. Tie with string in 2 or 3 places. Place stuffed tenderloins in a shallow roasting pan along with ¼ cup (50 mL) of the water. Place bacon on top. Bake, uncovered, for approximately 45 minutes to 1 hour or until meat is tender. Remove tenderloins to a warm serving platter. Make a paste with flour and 2 tablespoons (25 mL) of the water. Add remaining water to pan juices; bring to a boil, scraping the brown pieces clinging to the bottom of the pan. Lower heat; stir in flour paste. Add remaining cranberry sauce; simmer until sauce is creamy. Serve with meat. Garnish with parsley.

Serves 4

* Substitute dried apricots (soaked overnight in water or gin, then drained) for the prunes; use bottled lingonberries instead of cranberry sauce.

Scallopini of Veal with Roquefort, Rosemary and Sun-Dried Tomatoes

Perfect for an intimate dinner for two!

2	veal scallops	2
	Freshly ground pepper	
1	teaspoon butter	5 mL
1	teaspoon julienne sun-dried tomatoes	5 mL
1	tablespoon chopped shallots	15 mL
3	tablespoons white wine or vermouth	50 mL
¼	cup whipping cream	50 mL
1	teaspoon fresh rosemary leaves	5 mL
	(or ½ teaspoon/2 mL crushed dried)	
1	tablespoon crumbled Roquefort cheese	15 mL

Sprinkle veal with pepper. Melt butter in a fry pan over moderate heat. Sauté veal for 2 to 3 minutes or until lightly browned and just cooked. Place veal on two warmed dinner plates; place in a warm oven. In same pan, lightly sauté sun-dried tomatoes and shallots. Add wine, cream and rosemary. Boil to reduce by half. Stir in ½ of the Roquefort; pour over veal. Top with remaining Roquefort.

Serves 2

Veal with Artichokes and Mushrooms

3	pounds veal, cut into serving pieces	1.5	kg
¾	teaspoon salt	4	mL
¼	teaspoon pepper	1	mL
½	teaspoon paprika	2	mL
⅓	cup butter or margarine	75	mL
1	can (14 oz/398 mL) artichoke hearts, drained	1	
2	cups sliced mushrooms	500	mL
2	tablespoons all-purpose flour	25	mL
⅔	cup chicken broth	150	mL
3	tablespoons white wine	50	mL
¼	teaspoon dried rosemary	1	mL

Preheat oven to 350° F (180° C). Sprinkle veal with salt, pepper and paprika. Melt butter in a large fry pan over medium heat. Sauté veal until lightly brown; remove with a slotted spoon to a casserole dish. Arrange artichokes between veal pieces. In same fry pan, lightly sauté mushrooms until all liquid evaporates. Sprinkle flour over mushrooms; stir in broth, wine and rosemary. Cook, stirring, until slightly thickened. Pour over veal and artichokes. Cover and bake for 20 minutes or until tender.

Serves 8

* Boneless chicken will be equally as tasty in this recipe. Watch closely, though, so you don't overcook it.

Veal Scallopini in Tomato-Mushroom Sauce

Serve with pasta and a crisp green salad.

2	tablespoons butter	25	mL
1	cup finely chopped onion	250	mL
1	cup thinly sliced mushrooms	250	mL
4-5	tomatoes, peeled, seeded and chopped	4-5	
	Salt and pepper to taste		
¼	cup finely chopped fresh parsley	50	mL
	Basil, rosemary and tarragon to taste		
6-8	thin pieces veal scallopini	6-8	
	All-purpose flour		
2	tablespoons olive oil	25	mL
	Grated gruyère cheese		

In a large saucepan, melt butter. Sauté onion until transparent. Add mushrooms; cook briefly; add tomatoes, salt, pepper and herbs. Simmer, uncovered, until sauce has thickened, about 30 minutes. The sauce can be prepared the day before. Dredge veal in flour. Heat olive oil in a large skillet; brown veal for 1 to 2 minutes. Preheat oven to 400° F (200° C). Place veal pieces in a 13" x 9" (3.5 L) baking dish. Spoon tomato-mushroom sauce over veal. Cover tightly; bake for 15 to 20 minutes. Remove cover, sprinkle with cheese and continue baking, uncovered, for approximately 10 minutes or until sauce is bubbling and cheese is melted.

Serves 6 to 8

* This could be made with very thin slices of boneless pork.

Lamb Stuffed with Spinach, Mint and Tomato

Wait until you taste this! Worthy of your best guests.

¼	cup butter	50	mL
1	small clove garlic, minced	1	
1½	cups soft bread crumbs	375	mL
1	package (12 oz/340 g) frozen spinach, thawed and squeezed dry	1	
½	cup chopped fresh mint	125	mL
3	tablespoons mint sauce	50	mL
½	teaspoon salt	2	mL
¼	teaspoon pepper	1	mL
	Pinch of nutmeg		
5	pounds leg of lamb, boned	2.5	kg
1	tablespoon butter	15	mL
2	tomatoes, peeled, seeded and chopped	2	
	Dry mustard		
	Crushed garlic		
	Freshly ground black pepper		
2	tablespoons all-purpose flour	25	mL
2	cups water or stock	500	mL

Preheat oven to 325° F (160° C). To make spinach stuffing, heat the ¼ cup (50 mL) butter in a skillet. Add garlic; sauté lightly. Add bread crumbs; cook, stirring gently, until lightly browned. Add spinach, tossing with crumbs for 1 minute. Remove from heat; add mint, mint sauce, salt, pepper and nutmeg, tossing together with a fork.

Lay lamb out flat; spread evenly with spinach mixture. To make tomato stuffing, melt the 1 tablespoon (15 mL) butter in the skillet. Add tomatoes; cooking gently just until hot. Spread tomatoes over spinach. Roll lamb around stuffing; tie securely in several places. Rub outside of roast with dry mustard, garlic and pepper. Place lamb in a shallow roasting pan. Roast, uncovered, for approximately 2 hours or until meat thermometer registers 160° F (70° C) for medium; 170° F (75° C) for well-done. Remove roast; place on hot platter. Chill drippings quickly by adding a few ice cubes to roasting pan. Remove and discard all but 2 tablespoons (25 mL) of fat. Place pan over heat; sprinkle with flour. Stir to blend. Add water; bring to a boil. Stir until sauce is thickened. Adjust seasonings. Serve with roast.

Serves 6 to 8

Leg of Lamb with Apricot Stuffing

Succulent either roasted or barbecued.

1	boned leg of lamb	1	
Marinade			
1	cup red wine	250	mL
½	cup soy sauce	125	mL
Stuffing			
1	cup dried apricots	250	mL
¾	cup fresh bread crumbs	175	mL
½	cup chopped onion	125	mL
½	cup slivered almonds, toasted	125	mL
½	teaspoon dried savory	2	mL
½	teaspoon salt	2	mL
¼	teaspoon pepper	1	mL
1	egg, beaten	1	

Combine marinade ingredients. Place lamb and marinade in a plastic bag; refrigerate for 2 days, turning bag frequently. To prepare stuffing, cover apricots with boiling water. Soak for 2 to 3 hours; drain and cut into small pieces. Mix with remaining stuffing ingredients. Drain and reserve marinade from lamb. Stuff lamb; tie securely.

Preheat oven to 350° F (180° C). For medium-rare, roast, uncovered, for 1½ hours or until meat thermometer registers 150° F (60° C). Baste occasionally with reserved marinade while roasting. Let stand for 15 minutes before removing strings and slicing. If desired, juices can be thickened and served with lamb. Lamb can also be cooked on the barbecue.

Serves 6 to 8

Grilled Pepper Shrimps

¼	cup whole black peppercorns, freshly cracked	50	mL
20	medium to large fresh shrimps, shelled and deveined with tails intact	20	

Marinade

⅔	cup extra virgin olive oil	150	mL
⅓	cup rice vinegar	75	mL
1	teaspoon Dijon mustard or Sassy Sauce (see page 193)	5	mL
1	clove garlic, minced	1	
½	teaspoon Beau Monde or ground celery seed	2	mL
¼	cup soy sauce	50	mL

To crack pepper, place in a heavy plastic bag and crack with a hammer or the back of a heavy fry pan. Place cracked pepper on a shallow plate. Gently press each shrimp into the pepper. Shake the loose particles away, leaving a light covering. (Leave more on if your company is the "peppery" kind.) Mix all marinade ingredients in a glass bowl. Add peppered shrimps; marinate for a maximum of 2 hours at room temperature or longer in the refrigerator. Shrimps will begin to fall apart if left in the marinade too long. Barbecue shrimps over medium heat for about 5 minutes, turning frequently, until shrimps turn pink. Do not overcook!

Serves 4

Barbecued Shrimp with Two Marinades

Either marinade will give you a superb shrimp treat.

| 20 | medium to large fresh shrimps, shelled and deveined with tails intact | 20 | |

Orange-Sesame Marinade

3	tablespoons orange juice concentrate	50	mL
1	teaspoon sesame oil	5	mL
	Freshly ground pepper		

Balsamic Vinegar and Garlic Marinade

2	tablespoons olive oil	25	mL
1½	teaspoons balsamic vinegar	7	mL
½	teaspoon Worcestershire sauce	2	mL
1	clove garlic, minced	1	
	Pinch of cayenne		

Mix ingredients for marinade of choice in a glass bowl. Add shrimps; toss to coat. Marinate for 1 hour at room temperature. Barbecue over medium heat for about 5 minutes, turning frequently, until shrimps are pink. Do not overcook.

Serves 4

Grilled Seafood Satays with Peanut-Coconut Sauce

The sauce is to die for!

18	scallops	18
18	large shrimps, shelled and deveined	18
6	bamboo skewers, soaked in water for at least 30 minutes just before serving	6

Marinade

2	tablespoons finely chopped fresh ginger	25	mL
2	cloves garlic, minced	2	
½	cup vegetable oil	125	mL
2	teaspoons Chinese hot chili sauce	10	mL
¼	cup finely chopped green onions	50	mL
2	limes, grated rind and juice	2	

Peanut Sauce

½	cup finely chopped onion	125	mL
2	cloves garlic, minced	2	
2	teaspoons finely chopped fresh ginger	10	mL
2	tablespoons vegetable oil	25	mL
1	teaspoon Chinese hot chili sauce (or more to taste)	5	mL
½	cup peanut butter	125	mL
2	tablespoons soy sauce	25	mL
¼	cup lemon juice	50	mL
2	teaspoons sesame oil	10	mL
1	cup canned coconut milk	250	mL

Place scallops and shrimps in a large plastic bag. Combine all marinade ingredients; add marinade to scallops and shrimps. Marinate for 45 minutes.

Meanwhile, to prepare sauce, sauté onion, garlic and ginger in oil over medium heat for 2 minutes. Mix in chili sauce, peanut butter, soy sauce, lemon juice, sesame oil and coconut milk. Stir and simmer until smooth. Set aside.

Thread seafood alternately on skewers; brush with marinade. Grill over medium heat, turning once, for 4 to 5 minutes or until shrimps are pink. Do not overcook. Remove from barbecue; lightly brush with peanut sauce. Pass remaining sauce.

Serves 6

* Add 2 hot chilies to sauce if you enjoy the heat.

* Chicken cubes may be substituted for seafood.

Baked Stuffed Shrimps

40-48	jumbo shrimps	40-48	
36	Ritz crackers	36	
½	cup butter, melted	125	mL
1	can (7 oz/200 g) crab meat, drained	1	
2	tablespoons chopped fresh parsley	25	mL
1	teaspoon seasoned salt	5	mL

Preheat oven to 350° F (180° C). Peel and devein shrimps; cut down back so they lie flat. Place shrimps on a greased cookie sheet; set aside. In a blender or food processor, crush crackers to fine crumbs. In a bowl, combine cracker crumbs, butter, crab meat, parsley and seasoned salt. Place approximately 2 tablespoons (25 mL) of stuffing on each shrimp. Bake for 10 to 15 minutes.

Serves 8 to 10

* Recipe can easily be halved.

Island Baked Fish

Try serving with our Spiced Rice (see page 136)!

1½	pounds cod or other white fish	750	g

Marinade

½	cup water	125	mL
2	ounces creamed coconut	50	g
1	tablespoon peanut butter	15	mL
2	tablespoons peanut oil	25	mL
1	teaspoon salt	5	mL
	Juice and rind of 1 lime		
8	cardamom pods, crushed	8	
1	teaspoon turmeric	5	mL
1	piece (approximately 1"/2.5 cm long) fresh ginger, grated	1	
1-2	cloves garlic, minced	1-2	
2	green onions, sliced	2	

Cut fish into generous pieces; set aside. In a saucepan, bring water to a boil. Add creamed coconut; stir to dissolve. Reduce heat to low. Add peanut butter, oil and salt. Stir over low heat until mixture is smooth. Remove from heat. In a bowl, mix lime juice and rind, cardamom pods and turmeric. Add ginger, garlic, green onions and coconut mixture. Fold fish pieces carefully into marinade mixture. Cover and refrigerate for 2 to 12 hours.

Preheat oven to 375° F (190° C). Place fish, with the skin side down, in an ovenproof dish. Spoon marinade over fish. Cover and bake for 20 to 25 minutes.

Serves 4

Marinated Halibut Steaks

This recipe can be used for any white fish.

4-6	halibut steaks (1"/2.5 cm thick)	4-6

Marinade

½	cup orange juice	125 mL
⅓	cup soy sauce	75 mL
¼	cup ketchup	50 mL
2	tablespoons lemon juice	25 mL
¼	cup chopped fresh parsley	50 mL
2	cloves garlic, minced	2
½	teaspoon black pepper	2 mL

Arrange steaks in a single layer in a shallow pan. Combine remaining ingredients; pour over fish. Refrigerate for 1 to 2 hours, turning over at least once. Remove from refrigerator 30 minutes before cooking. Barbecue over high heat for approximately 5 to 8 minutes per side, basting frequently with the marinade.

Serves 4 to 6

Succulent Salmon

As good as it sounds.

2-6	salmon fillets or filleted salmon trout	2-6	

Marinade

½	cup olive or corn oil	125	mL
¼	cup lemon juice	50	mL
2-3	cloves garlic, minced	2-3	
¼	cup chopped fresh parsley	50	mL
	Chopped fresh parsley for garnish		
	Lemon wedges for garnish		

Mix oil, juice, garlic and the ¼ cup (50 mL) parsley together. Place fish fillets in an ovenproof baking dish, skin side up. Pour marinade over fish and marinate for up to 24 hours in the refrigerator. If marinating for just a few hours, do so at room temperature.

Preheat oven to 450° F-500° F (230° C-260° C). Turn fillets over just before baking. Baste liberally with marinade. Bake for 6 to 10 minutes, depending on the number of fillets. Baste from time to time. Fish is done when it flakes easily with a fork. Do not overcook! Garnish with parsley and lemon wedges.

Serves 2 to 6

* To use a whole 5- to 6-pound (2.5 kg) salmon, double the marinade ingredients; marinate for the same length of time. Bake at the same temperature for 10 to 14 minutes.

* Vary the marinade by adding 1½ teaspoons (7 mL) Dijon mustard, 2 tablespoons (25 mL) capers and cracked black pepper to taste.

* This marinade can be used for most fish.

* Just as delicious barbecued!

Swordfish Scallopini

Swordfish has the texture of veal and the appeal of fish.

2	pounds swordfish steaks, each sliced horizontally in half as for veal scallopini	1	kg
2	tablespoons all-purpose flour	25	mL
	Freshly ground black pepper to taste		

Kiwi and Lime Sauce

1	tablespoon butter	15	mL
1	tablespoon vegetable oil	15	mL
2	kiwis, peeled and sliced	2	
2	cups chicken broth	500	mL
1	lime, thinly sliced	1	

Preheat oven to 200° F (100° C). Have your fishmonger do the slicing of the swordfish. Place flour, pepper and swordfish slices in a plastic bag. Gently shake until fish is coated. Place a platter in oven to warm. In a fry pan, sauté fish in butter and oil for approximately 2 to 3 minutes on each side. Remove fish to heated platter; place a kiwi slice on each piece. Return platter to warm oven. Add chicken broth to fry pan; stir up drippings. Place sliced lime in pan; simmer for 5 to 7 minutes. Pour sauce over fish. Place lime slices on fish to garnish.

Serves 8

* For a change, try this:

Lemon and Caper Sauce: Follow the above directions, replacing the kiwi slices with 3 to 4 tablespoons (50 mL) capers. Sprinkle these on fish slices. Place lemon slices instead of lime in broth.

Fresh Tuna en Croûte

1½	pounds fresh tuna, sliced horizontally into two ½" (1.5 cm) slices	750 g
1	package (14 oz/397 g) frozen puff pastry, thawed	1
1	teaspoon mayonnaise	5 mL
	Salt and pepper to taste	
3-4	fresh sorrel leaves or watercress sprigs	3-4
1	egg yolk, mixed with 2 tablespoons (25 mL) water	1
	Watercress sprigs for garnish	

Trim the two slices of tuna into triangular shapes, discarding any black or fatty pieces. Roll pastry out on a lightly floured board. Cut pastry into two similar shapes approximately 1½" (3.5 cm) larger than the tuna pieces. Place 1 slice of tuna on 1 piece of pastry. Spread with mayonnaise and sprinkle with salt and pepper. Cover with pieces of sorrel. Top with second slice of tuna. Brush edges of pastry with egg yolk mixture. Cover with second piece of pastry; crimp top and bottom together with fork. Slightly elongate two ends of the triangle to give angel fish shape. Decorate top with a pastry eye and mouth using egg yolk wash to cement in place. Mark scales on surface using the edge of a 1" (2.5 cm) round cookie cutter. Lightly brush surface with egg yolk wash. Place fish on lightly greased cookie sheet; refrigerate until ready to bake. Preheat oven to 425° F (220° C). Bake for 15 minutes; reduce heat to 350° F (180° C) and bake for 15 minutes. Transfer to a serving platter. Garnish with watercress.

Serves 4 to 6

* Tuna not your favorite? Try swordfish, salmon or halibut.

Vegetables

Garlic Beans Three Ways

Simply delicious.

1	pound fresh green beans, diagonally cut or whole	500	g
4	teaspoons butter	20	mL
1	clove garlic, minced	1	

Wash and prepare beans. Place in a saucepan of boiling water; cook for 4 to 6 minutes, until tender-crisp. Drain beans in a sieve. Quickly place pan back on low heat. Add butter; melt. Add garlic; then beans. Toss.

Serves 4

* To prepare beans early in day, drain beans after boiling; quickly cool under cold water. Drain again and pat dry. At serving time, melt butter in a fry pan. Add garlic, then beans and cook only until beans are hot.

* Add either or both of the following:

4	slices bacon, crisply cooked and crumbled	4	
¼	cup pine nuts, toasted	50	mL

Cardamom Carrots

Colorful and zesty!

2	pounds carrots, peeled and diagonally sliced (¼"/5 mm thick)	1	kg
¼	cup unsalted butter	50	mL
4	teaspoons freshly grated orange rind	20	mL
8	cardamom pods, hulled and seeds pounded in a mortar (or ½-1 teaspoon/2-5 mL ground cardamom) Salt to taste	8	

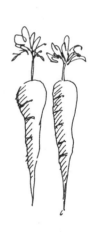

Steam carrots for 5 to 7 minutes or just until tender. Melt butter; add grated orange rind and cardamom. Toss carrots in butter mixture. Add salt to taste. Place in serving dish. May be prepared ahead and reheated over low heat.

Serves 8

Braised Herbed Cucumbers

An unusual way to use cucumbers in the winter, or to deal with a summer abundance.

2	English cucumbers or 4 regular cucumbers	2
1	tablespoon coarse salt	15 mL
1	tablespoon vinegar	15 mL
¼	cup butter, melted	50 mL
2	tablespoons snipped fresh dill	25 mL
2	tablespoons chopped fresh chives	25 mL
1	tablespoon minced shallots	15 mL
	White pepper to taste	
½	cup whipping cream	125 mL
	Fresh parsley or dill for garnish	

If using regular cucumbers, peel cucumbers, halve them lengthwise and, with a small spoon, scoop out the seeds. (This is not necessary with English cucumbers.) Cut into 1" x 1¼" (2.5 cm x 3 cm) pieces. Sprinkle with salt and vinegar; let stand for 2 to 3 hours at room temperature. Drain and pat dry.

Preheat oven to 375° F (190° C). Transfer cucumbers to a stove-to-oven dish; toss with butter, dill, chives, shallots and white pepper. Bake for 20 minutes or until barely tender. Remove from oven; add cream. Toss; cook over medium heat for about 5 minutes or until cream is reduced and thickened. Sprinkle with minced parsley for garnish.

Serves 6 to 8

Onion Lover's Onions

If you like onions, you'll love these!

4	cooking onions, thinly sliced	4
2	tablespoons butter	25 mL
1-2	tablespoons brown sugar	15-25 mL
4	teaspoons balsamic vinegar or water	20 mL
	Salt and pepper to taste	

Preheat oven to 300° F (150° C). Spread onions in a roasting pan or rectangular baking dish. Dot with butter; sprinkle with brown sugar, balsamic vinegar, salt and pepper. Cover tightly; bake for 50 to 60 minutes, stirring once. This can be stored in refrigerator up to 5 days. Serve hot or cold or as below.

Makes about 2 cups (500 mL)

* Use as

• a pizza topping

• an accompaniment to sautéed liver, sausage or other meats

• a hamburger condiment

• an addition to spinach or other vegetables for extra flavor

Sweet Pepper Sauté
Quick and versatile.

1	tablespoon olive oil	15 mL
1	clove garlic, minced	1
1	sweet red pepper, julienne	1
1	sweet yellow pepper, julienne	1
1	sweet green pepper, julienne	1
2	teaspoons balsamic vinegar	10 mL
	Salt and freshly ground black pepper to taste	

Heat olive oil and garlic in a heavy fry pan or wok over medium to medium-high heat. Do not let garlic burn. Add julienne peppers all at once; sauté quickly just until tender, but still crisp. Add balsamic vinegar, salt and pepper. Serve immediately or at room temperature.

Serves 4

* Not only good as a vegetable, but wonderful as a condiment. Try it on a roast beef or chicken sandwich, over a hamburger or tossed into a green salad.

Grilled Vegetables
Cook ahead for a relaxed barbecue.

Vegetables of your choice
Marinade and baste
½	cup extra virgin olive oil	125	mL
2	tablespoons balsamic vinegar	25	mL
2	cloves garlic, minced	2	
2	tablespoons chopped fresh basil	25	mL
	Extra basil for garnish		

Early in the day, combine oil, vinegar, garlic and the 2 tablespoons (25 mL) basil in a jar; let stand at room temperature to blend flavors. Choose vegetables from the following or use your own favorites: sweet peppers of any color, eggplant, zucchini, summer squash, red or Spanish onion, Belgian endive, thick tomato slices or parboiled potatoes or sweet potatoes. Cut all vegetables in large, thick slices. For example, cut eggplant and zucchini into lengthwise quarters. Cut peppers into halves or quarters, and onions into ½" (1.5 cm) slices. Smaller pieces will fall through the grill.

One hour before cooking time, brush marinade on both sides of the prepared vegetables and let marinate. Heat grill to medium-low; grill each vegetable, basting occasionally, until cooked to your liking. Garnish with additional chopped basil or basil sprigs. Serve hot or at room temperature. Leftovers are equally good the next day.

Serves as many as you like

* Try your own favorite vinaigrette or simply use oil flavored as you like it.

* Use grilled vegetables in tossed salads.

* After grilling, cut vegetables into smaller pieces and serve as an hors d'oeuvre with a dip if desired.

* Add to a roast beef or chicken sandwich.

* Create a Mediterranean vegetable pita sandwich by using an assortment of grilled vegetables and dress with plain yogurt or yogurt flavored with chopped onion, garlic and lots of freshly ground black pepper.

Sherried Tomatoes

6	tomatoes	6
6	tablespoons sherry	90 mL
1½	teaspoons dillweed	7 mL
	Freshly ground black pepper	
6	tablespoons mayonnaise	90 mL
6	tablespoons grated Cheddar cheese	90 mL

Turn oven to broil. Remove core from each tomato; cut tomatoes in half horizontally. Place, cut side up, on a cookie sheet or in a muffin tin. Pierce cut surface several times with a fork to allow sherry to penetrate. Sprinkle each tomato half with sherry, dill and pepper. Broil for 2 to 3 minutes. (May be prepared to this point 1 hour before serving.) Mix mayonnaise and cheese together; spread over tomatoes. Broil again for 2 to 3 minutes until bubbly and browned. Serve immediately.

Serves 6

Scalloped Tomatoes

Old-fashioned comfort food — perfect for winter suppers.

1	cup chopped celery	250	mL
½	cup chopped onion	125	mL
1	clove garlic, minced	1	
2	tablespoons butter	25	mL
2	tablespoons all-purpose flour	25	mL
3	slices toast, cubed	3	
1	can (14 oz/398 mL) stewed tomatoes	1	
1	tablespoon granulated sugar	15	mL
¼	cup chopped fresh basil	50	mL
1	teaspoon salt	5	mL
2	teaspoons Dijon mustard	10	mL
	Freshly ground black pepper		
2	tablespoons freshly grated Parmesan cheese	25	mL

Preheat oven to 350° F (180° C). In a fry pan, sauté celery, onion and garlic in butter until tender. Blend in flour. Add remaining ingredients, except Parmesan and half of the toast cubes. Place mixture in 1 quart (1 L) casserole. Sprinkle remaining toast cubes and Parmesan cheese over the top. Bake for 25 minutes until topping browns and mixture is bubbling.

Serves 4

Sautéed Cherry Tomatoes

Sometimes the easiest things are the best.

1-2	tablespoons pesto	15-25 mL
1	pint cherry tomatoes	500 mL
	Pinch of granulated sugar	
	Lots of freshly ground pepper	

Heat pesto in a fry pan over medium-high heat. When hot, add tomatoes. Sprinkle with sugar. Sauté and toss until tomatoes are heated through and coated with pesto. Do not let tomatoes burst. Season generously with pepper.

Serves 4

* Instead of pesto, sauté tomatoes in butter or olive oil. Sprinkle with chopped fresh basil or your favorite fresh herbs.

* Sauté 1 minced onion in 1 tablespoon (15 mL) butter until soft. Add tomatoes and sauté until warm. Add 1 teaspoon (5 mL) brown sugar and 1 teaspoon (5 mL) dried basil.

* Sauté 1 minced clove garlic with ¼ cup (50 mL) bread crumbs in 1-2 tablespoons (15-25 mL) butter until lightly toasted. Toss with sautéed cherry tomatoes.

Butternut Squash Supreme
Glazed to perfection.

1	large butternut squash, peeled and cubed (about 6 cups/1.5 L)	1	
½	cup chopped pecans	125	mL
2	tablespoons butter	25	mL
3	tablespoons 10% cream	50	mL
1	tablespoon brown sugar	15	mL
¼	teaspoon salt	1	mL
¼	teaspoon pepper	1	mL
	Pinch of nutmeg		
1	teaspoon grated fresh ginger (or ¼ teaspoon/1 mL ground ginger)	5	mL

Glaze
1	tablespoon butter	15	mL
3	tablespoons light corn syrup	50	mL
2	tablespoons brown sugar	25	mL
¼	cup chopped pecans	50	mL

Preheat oven to 350° F (180° C). Cook squash in boiling, salted water for approximately 20 minutes or until soft; mash. Add pecans, butter, cream, brown sugar, salt, pepper, nutmeg and ginger. Place in a casserole dish.

For glaze, melt butter; add corn syrup, brown sugar and pecans. Toss lightly; spread on top of squash mixture. This casserole can be made a day in advance but add the glaze just before baking. Bake for 20 minutes or until a glaze forms.

Serves 4 to 6

Squash and Sweet Potato Casserole

A great combination.

1	pound sweet potatoes, peeled and cubed (about 3½ cups/875 mL)	500	g
1	butternut squash, peeled and cubed (about 4 cups/1 L)	1	
1	large Spy apple, peeled and cubed (about 1½ cups/375 mL)	1	
1	cup tart apple juice or water	250	mL
¾	teaspoon salt	4	mL
2	tablespoons butter	25	mL
¾	teaspoon grated fresh ginger (or ¼ teaspoon/1 mL ground) Freshly ground black pepper to taste	4	mL

In a large saucepan, combine sweet potatoes, squash, apple, apple juice and salt. Boil gently for 30 minutes or until tender. Drain if necessary. Add butter, ginger and pepper. Purée in a food processor or whip with a beater until smooth. This dish can be prepared in advance or frozen until needed. To reheat, place covered casserole in preheated (350° F /180° C) oven for 35 to 40 minutes or until heated through.

Serves 8

Rutabaga with Honey and Mint
Cooked this way, the lowly rutabaga is divine!

1	small rutabaga, peeled and cut in strips	1
¼-⅓	cup butter	50-75 mL
2	tablespoons honey	25 mL
¼	cup chopped fresh mint leaves	50 mL
	Pepper to taste	

Cook rutabaga in boiling, salted water until tender. Drain. Toss with butter, honey, chopped mint and pepper.

Serves 4 to 6

French Peas
A classic.

4	teaspoons butter	20 mL
½	head iceberg lettuce	½
2	cups frozen green peas	500 mL
½	teaspoon granulated sugar	2 mL
3	green onions, chopped	3
1	tablespoon water	15 mL
1	teaspoon chopped fresh rosemary (or ¼ teaspoon/1 mL dried)	5 mL
1	clove garlic, minced	1
	Freshly ground black pepper	
	Pinch of flour	
	Salt to taste	

Melt butter in saucepan. Slice lettuce in long shreds. Add ½ of the lettuce to butter in pan. Top with the next 8 ingredients; spread remaining lettuce on top. Cover and bring to a boil. Lower heat; simmer for 15 minutes, stirring 2 to 3 times.

Serves 4

Two Ways with New Potatoes

New potatoes to serve 8

Scrub potatoes; cook in boiling, salted water until tender. Drain; serve tossed with one of the following sauces.

Savory Sauce

¼	cup butter	50 mL
2	tablespoons olive oil	25 mL
1	lemon, juice and grated rind	1
	Pinch of flour	
	Pinch of freshly grated or ground nutmeg	
	Salt to taste	
	Freshly ground black pepper	
2	tablespoons chopped fresh chives	25 mL
3	tablespoons chopped fresh parsley	50 mL

In a small saucepan, heat butter, oil, lemon rind, lemon juice and flour. Bring to a boil and cook for 1 minute. Remove from heat; stir in remaining ingredients. Toss immediately with hot new potatoes.

Chive and Mint Sauce

	Sea salt to taste	
¼	cup fresh mint	50 mL
2	tablespoons chopped fresh chives	25 mL
6	tablespoons butter, melted	75 mL
	Sour cream or yogurt (optional)	

Sprinkle sea salt on mint and chives; chop together. Toss hot new potatoes with mint mixture and butter. Serve with sour cream or yogurt (if using).

Serves 8

Lentil and Rice Casserole

Healthy and hearty.

8	slices side bacon, chopped	8	
1	cup chopped onion	250	mL
2	cloves garlic, minced	2	
1	tablespoon vegetable oil (if required)	15	mL
1	cup brown or green lentils	250	mL
¾	cup brown rice	175	mL
1	large carrot, finely diced	1	
4	cups beef broth	1 L	
1	teaspoon dried thyme	5	mL
1	teaspoon dried basil	5	mL
½	teaspoon dried oregano	2	mL
	Salt and pepper to taste		
⅓	cup chopped fresh parsley	75	mL

Preheat oven to 350° F (180° C). In a large 10-cup (2.5 L) stove-to-oven casserole, fry chopped bacon until browned. Remove bacon with a slotted spoon, drain and set aside. Add onion and garlic to the bacon fat; sauté until lightly browned, adding a tablespoon of oil if needed. Add lentils, brown rice and carrot, stirring until well coated with oil. Add broth and seasonings, except parsley. Bake, covered, for 45 minutes or until liquid is absorbed and rice and lentils are cooked. Stir in chopped parsley just before serving.

Serves 6

* For a meatless casserole, replace bacon with 3 tablespoons (50 mL) oil.

* For a different taste, replace thyme, basil and oregano with 1 teaspoon (5 mL) each of cinnamon and cumin and a pinch of cayenne. Add 1 cup (250 mL) of chopped, mixed, dried apricots and prunes. Add ½ cup (125 mL) of diced, peeled apple 10 minutes before the casserole is done.

* Leftovers can be combined with canned tomatoes and reheated for another taste.

Spiced Rice

Gives added punch to pork or chicken dishes.

1	cup long-grain rice	250	mL
1	piece (approximately 1"/2.5 cm long) fresh ginger, peeled	1	
2	cups boiling water or chicken broth	500	mL
¼	cup raisins	50	mL
¼	cup currants	50	mL
¼	cup chopped apricots, prunes or both Freshly ground black pepper to taste	50	mL
½	teaspoon nutmeg	2	mL
2	tablespoons chopped green onions	25	mL
1	tablespoon lemon juice	15	mL
1	teaspoon ground coriander	5	mL
1	tablespoon olive oil Toasted pine nuts for garnish	15	mL

Simmer rice with ginger piece in the boiling water for 20 to 30 minutes or until tender. Drain; remove ginger from rice. Meanwhile, cover fruits with hot water. Drain when plump (about 10 minutes). Add pepper, nutmeg, green onions, lemon juice, coriander and oil to rice. Gently fold in fruits. Garnish with pine nuts.

Serves 4 to 6

* Plan to make more than you need because leftovers are a treat served cold as a salad.

Breads

Gammy's Tea Biscuits

These biscuits, served with one of the flavored butters that follow, are a heart-warming treat!

2	cups all-purpose flour	500	mL
2	teaspoons sugar	10	mL
½	teaspoon salt	2	mL
½	teaspoon cream of tartar	2	mL
4	teaspoons baking powder	20	mL
½	cup shortening	125	mL
1	egg	1	
⅔	cup (approximately) milk	150	mL

Preheat oven to 400° F (200° C). Sift dry ingredients into a large mixing bowl. Cut in shortening with a pastry blender or two knives until mixture resembles coarse meal. Break egg into a 1-cup (250 mL) measure; stir with a fork. Fill the cup with milk; stir to mix. Make a well in the center of the dry ingredients; add the milk mixture all at once. With a fork, stir quickly just until moistened. Mixture should be sticky. Using a spatula, scoop out mixture onto a flour-covered board. With floured hands, knead GENTLY 12 times until a smooth soft ball forms. With hands, flatten ball into a circle, 1" (2.5 cm) thick. Cut into rounds with a floured biscuit cutter; place rounds on a greased baking sheet. Bake for approximately 15 minutes until light brown on top. Remove from oven and place a clean, dry tea towel over biscuits to keep them soft. Serve warm.

Makes 12 to 16 biscuits

Variations

* Herb and Cheese Biscuits: Add ½ cup (125 mL) grated Parmesan and old Cheddar (mixed) and ¼-½ cup (50-125 mL) mixed chopped chives, parsley and basil to biscuit mixture.

* Lemon Biscuits: Add a pinch of baking soda to the dry ingredients and 1 tablespoon (15 mL) lemon juice and 1 teaspoon (5 mL) grated lemon rind to liquid. Currants or raisins may also be added to lemon biscuits.

* Cinnamon Pinwheel: Flatten biscuit mixture into a rectangle. Spread with butter; sprinkle with brown sugar, cinnamon and/or raisins. Roll like a jelly roll, pinching edge to seal. Cut into pinwheels and bake.

* Pot-Pie Topping: Place small biscuits touching on top of a bubbling beef or chicken stew. Bake at 400° F (200° C) until top is brown and firm to touch.

* Cheese Biscuits: Add ½ cup (125 mL) grated old Cheddar cheese to biscuit mixture.

* Raisin Biscuits: Add ½ cup (125 mL) raisins or currants to biscuit mixture.

A Quintet of Butters

Two sweet and three savory butters to complement Gammy's Tea Biscuits. Sweet butters are also nice with pancakes or waffles.

STRAWBERRY BUTTER

½	cup butter	125 mL
½	cup chopped fresh strawberries	125 mL
2	tablespoons strawberry jam	25 mL
	fresh whole strawberry for garnish	

LEMON BUTTER

½	cup butter	125 mL
2	tablespoons lemon conserve	25 mL
1	tablespoon fresh lemon juice	15 mL
	Zest of ½ lemon	
	Thin lemon slice for garnish	

HERBED BUTTER

½	cup butter	125 mL
1	tablespoon chopped fresh rosemary	15 mL
1	tablespoon chopped fresh tarragon	15 mL
2	tablespoons chopped fresh chives	25 mL
2	tablespoons chopped fresh parsley	25 mL
1	small clove garlic, minced	1
	Freshly ground pepper	
	A sprig of an herb for garnish	

RED PEPPER BUTTER

½	cup butter	125 mL
2	tablespoons Roasted Red Pepper Sauce (see page 192)	25 mL
1	teaspoon minced onion or chives	5 mL
1	tablespoon chopped fresh basil	15 mL

SMOKED HAM BUTTER

½	cup unsalted butter	125 mL
1	cup ground smoked ham	250 mL
2	tablespoons chopped chives	25 mL

Whip butter in a food processor or by hand. Add one of the above combinations (excluding garnish); mix until light and fluffy. Place in a small crock or ramekin; garnish.

Makes about ½ cup (125 mL)

Irish Oatmeal Bread

Easy to make just before a meal.

3	cups sifted all-purpose flour	750 mL
1¼	cups large-flake rolled oats	300 mL
4	teaspoons baking powder	20 mL
1	teaspoon salt	5 mL
1	tablespoon soft butter	15 mL
1	egg	1
¼	cup honey	50 mL
1½	cups milk	375 mL

Preheat oven to 350° F (180° C). Grease a 9" x 5" (2 L) loaf pan. Mix dry ingredients in a mixing bowl. In a separate bowl, mix butter, egg, honey and milk; add to dry ingredients. Combine until moist. Pour into pan; bake for about 70 minutes or until golden brown. Let cool for a few minutes. Turn out onto rack. Serve immediately.

Makes 1 loaf

Corn Bread

1	cup all-purpose flour (unsifted)	250	mL
⅔	cup cornmeal	150	mL
½	cup corn flour	125	mL
¼	cup granulated sugar	50	mL
4	teaspoons baking powder	20	mL
½	teaspoon salt	2	mL
1⅓	cup milk	325	mL
5	tablespoons melted butter or vegetable oil	75	mL
1	egg, lightly beaten	1	

Preheat oven to 350° F (180° C). Grease a 9" (2.5 L) square cake pan or 12 muffin tins. Sift dry ingredients together in a large bowl. Combine moist ingredients separately; add all at once to the dry ingredients. Stir just until moistened. Turn into baking pan; bake for 25 to 30 minutes.

Makes 1 pan or 12 muffins

Try one of these additions.
* ¾ cup (175 mL) small cubes Cheddar cheese
scattered on top
* 1 cup (250 mL) blueberries
* 3 tablespoons (50 mL) chopped jalapeño peppers
mixed with 3 tablespoons (50 mL) sautéed chopped onion

Carrot-Pineapple Muffins

⅔	cup granulated sugar	150	mL
⅔	cup vegetable oil	150	mL
2	eggs, beaten	2	
1½	cups all-purpose flour	375	mL
2	teaspoons baking powder	10	mL
1	teaspoon baking soda	5	mL
1	teaspoon cinnamon	5	mL
½	teaspoon salt	2	mL
1	teaspoon vanilla	5	mL
1	cup finely grated carrots	250	mL
1	cup drained crushed pineapple	250	mL

Preheat oven to 375° F (190° C). In a bowl, combine sugar, oil and eggs. In another bowl, combine dry ingredients; mix well. Add dry ingredients to egg mixture; stir just to moisten. Add vanilla, carrots and pineapple. Fill greased muffin tins to top; bake for 20 minutes.

Makes 12 large muffins

Pumpkin Muffins

¾	cup corn oil	175	mL
1	cup brown sugar	250	mL
2	eggs	2	
1	cup canned pumpkin purée	250	mL
½	cup raisins (optional)	125	mL
½	cup chopped nuts (optional)	125	mL
⅓	cup milk	75	mL
1½	cups all-purpose flour	375	mL
1½	teaspoons baking powder	7	mL
1	teaspoon baking soda	5	mL
½	teaspoon salt	2	mL
1	teaspoon cinnamon	5	mL
¼	teaspoon cloves	1	mL
¼	teaspoon ground nutmeg	1	mL
¼	teaspoon ground ginger	1	mL

Preheat oven to 350° F (180° C). Blend together first 6 ingredients. Add milk; stirring as little as possible. In another bowl, combine remaining ingredients; add to wet mixture. Place in greased or paper-lined muffin tins. Bake for 20 to 25 minutes, checking to make sure they do not overbake.

Makes at least 12 large muffins

Sweet Potato Yeast Rolls

The color AND taste of these rolls — beautiful!

¼	cup lukewarm water	50	mL
2	teaspoons granulated sugar	10	mL
2	teaspoons (1 pkg) dry yeast	10	mL
1	cup mashed sweet potatoes (freshly cooked)	250	mL
1	cup milk, scalded	250	mL
¼	cup butter	50	mL
3	tablespoons granulated sugar	50	mL
1½	teaspoons salt	7	mL
½	teaspoon ground nutmeg	2	mL
2	large eggs, beaten	2	
4½-5	cups all-purpose flour	1.12-1.25	L

Mix lukewarm water with the 2 teaspoons (10 mL) sugar in a small bowl. Sprinkle yeast over the top. Let stand undisturbed for 15 to 20 minutes in a warm place. In a large mixing bowl, combine sweet potatoes, milk, butter, the 3 tablespoons (50 mL) sugar, salt and nutmeg. Let cool to lukewarm. Stir in beaten eggs and 2 cups (500 mL) of the flour. Beat with an electric mixer or by hand until dough is smooth and elastic. Stir yeast mixture; add to dough. Stir by hand while adding more flour until dough is stiff. Turn dough out on a floured board; knead 200 times, adding more flour until dough is smooth, elastic and no longer sticky. Grease top of dough; place in a greased mixing bowl. Cover with a tea towel and put in a warm place until double in volume, about 1 hour. Punch down dough; let rest 10 minutes. Turn dough out onto a floured board; shape into rolls. Place rolls side by side, on a well-greased baking sheet or in greased muffin pans. Let rise in a warm place until double in volume, 35 minutes to 1 hour.

Preheat oven to 375° F (190° C). Bake for 10 to 12 minutes.

Makes 24 to 36

Soft Fennel Breadsticks

A fast yeast bread to serve with Italian food. Can be made in 1½ hours, start to finish!

4-5	cups all-purpose flour (reserve 1 cup/250 mL)	1-1.25	L
1	tablespoon granulated sugar	15	mL
2	teaspoons (1 pkg) fast-rising yeast	10	mL
1½	teaspoons salt	7	mL
1	tablespoon fennel seed	15	mL
2	cups water	500	mL
¼	cup vegetable oil	50	mL
1	egg yolk mixed with 2 teaspoons (10 mL) water for glaze	1	

Place part of the flour, sugar, yeast, salt and fennel seeds in a large mixing bowl. Heat water and oil to 125° F (60° C) or until your finger can just stand it. (Fast-rising yeast requires hotter water than traditional yeast.) Add water and oil to dry ingredients; mix well. Flour a board with reserved flour; turn dough out onto it. Knead 200 times, working in extra flour as needed, until dough is smooth and elastic and no stickiness remains. Allow dough to rest, covered, on board for 10 minutes. Roll out on floured board to a 12" x 15" (30 cm x 40 cm) rectangle, about ½" (1.5 cm) thick. Cut into 1" x 4" (2.5 cm x 10 cm) logs with a sharp knife. Place logs on greased baking pans. Cover with a dry towel and let rise in a warm place, until double in volume, about 30 to 45 minutes. To speed up rising time, place baking pans over pans of boiling water.

Preheat oven to 400° F (200° C). Brush dough with egg glaze; bake until light brown, about 14 minutes.

Makes about 36

* To make plain bread sticks, omit fennel.

* To make French sticks, cut rectangle into 2 or 3 strips and shape into long loaves. Bake 25 to 30 minutes or until loaves sound hollow when tapped.

Grain and Seed Bread with Raisins and Orange

A meal in every slice.

½	cup lukewarm water	125	mL
1	teaspoon granulated sugar	5	mL
2	teaspoons (1 package) dry yeast	10	mL
1½	cups orange juice	375	mL
⅓	cup cornmeal	75	mL
¼	cup butter or lard	50	mL
⅓	cup molasses	75	mL
	Rind of 1 orange, grated		
1	teaspoon salt	5	mL
⅔	cup raisins, plumped in water	150	mL
½	cup sunflower seeds	125	mL
¼	cup sesame seeds	50	mL
½	cup oat bran	125	mL
½	cup rolled oats	125	mL
2	tablespoons flaxseed	25	mL
¼	cup chopped almonds, toasted	50	mL
1	egg	1	
1	cup whole-wheat flour	250	mL
2-3	cups all-purpose flour	500-750	mL
	Seeds or rolled oats for garnish		

Dissolve sugar in lukewarm water. Sprinkle yeast on top; let stand in a warm place for 15 to 20 minutes. Pour orange juice into a saucepan. Use wooden spoon to stir in cornmeal. Cook over medium heat until mixture is thick and smooth, about 5 minutes. Remove from heat; stir in butter immediately. When melted, stir in molasses, orange rind and salt. Let cool to room temperature. Stir in plumped raisins, sunflower seeds, sesame seeds, oat bran, rolled oats, flaxseed and almonds. Slightly beat egg with fork; divide egg, reserving half for glazing. Stir remaining ½ egg into the seed mixture. Stir in yeast mixture. Add whole-wheat flour and part of the all-purpose flour. Knead 200 times on a floured board, adding more flour until dough is smooth, elastic and no longer sticky. Return to mixing bowl and grease top of dough; cover with a dry towel. Let rise in a warm place until double in volume, about 1 hour. Punch down and let rest 10 minutes. Form into 4 small loaves; place in greased bread pans. Cover with a dry towel and let rise until double in volume. Brush with reserved egg glaze; sprinkle seeds on top. Preheat oven to 375° F (190° C). Bake for about 20 minutes until loaf sounds hollow when tapped. Remove from pan; let cool on a rack.

Makes 4 small loaves

* To make this loaf without an orange flavor, replace orange juice with water, and eliminate the orange rind.

* Eliminate some of the seeds if you don't have them on hand.

Parmesan Puffs

A versatile snack or lunch addition.

½	cup milk	125 mL
½	cup water	125 mL
½	cup butter	125 mL
1	cup all-purpose flour	250 mL
3	eggs	3
1½	cups freshly grated Parmesan cheese	375 mL
½	teaspoon pepper	2 mL
2	tablespoons chopped fresh tarragon or fresh dill	25 mL

Preheat oven to 400° F (200° C). In heavy saucepan, mix milk, water and butter over high heat until butter melts. Add flour all at once; beat well until mixture leaves sides of pan and forms a ball. Let cool to warm temperature; add eggs one at a time, whisking after each egg until well blended. Stir in Parmesan cheese and pepper. Add herb of choice. Drop by spoonful on greased cookie sheet. Bake for 20 minutes or until golden. For hors d'oeuvres, make smaller.

Makes 18 to 24 puffs; 36 to 48 hors d'oeuvres

Sesame Herb Toast

A tasty accompaniment to your favorite soup!

½	cup butter, softened	125	mL
4	tablespoons sesame seeds	50	mL
½	teaspoon dried marjoram	2	mL
2	tablespoons chopped fresh chives	25	mL
½	teaspoon dried basil or rosemary	2	mL
10-12	thin bread slices, crusts off	10-12	

Preheat oven to 325° F (160° C). Cream butter well. Add next four ingredients; combine well. Cut bread slices into thirds; spread with butter mixture. Bake, on a cookie sheet, for 15 minutes. Serve hot or at room temperature. May be frozen before or after baking.

Makes 30 to 36 pieces

Crisp Bread with Pine Nuts and Parmesan

1	package of refrigerated crescent rolls (8 rolls per package)	1	
3	tablespoons pine nuts	50	mL
	Vegetable oil		
2	tablespoons grated Parmesan cheese	25	mL

Preheat oven to 375° F (190° C). Open package of crescent rolls; separate into triangles. Place on a baking sheet. Press 1 teaspoon (5 mL) pine nuts firmly into each triangle. Brush with a little vegetable oil; sprinkle with Parmesan cheese. Bake for 5 minutes or until lightly browned. Serve warm.

Makes 8 golden triangle puffs

* Try replacing pine nuts with sesame or poppy seeds.

Desserts

Chocolate Cheesecake Extravaganza

Ribbons of sinful richness.

Crust

1	cup crushed chocolate wafers	250	mL
3	tablespoons melted butter	50	mL

Filling

3	packages (each 8 oz/250 g) cream cheese, softened	3	
⅔	cup sugar	150	mL
3	eggs	3	
1	teaspoon vanilla	5	mL
3	tablespoons peach liqueur	50	mL
⅔	cup semi-sweet chocolate chips, melted	150	mL

Frosting

½	cup whipping cream	125	mL
¾	cup semi-sweet chocolate chips	175	mL

Preheat oven to 350° F (180° C). Grease sides of a 9" (2.5 L) springform pan. For crust, combine wafer crumbs and butter; press into bottom of pan. Bake for 10 minutes. In a food processor or with a mixer, blend cream cheese and sugar. Add eggs, one at a time, mixing after each addition. Add vanilla; mix well. Pour ½ of the cheese mixture into another bowl; stir in liqueur. Add melted chocolate to remaining cheese mixture. Process briefly. Pour chocolate cheese over crust. Spoon peach cheese carefully over chocolate layer. Bake for 40 minutes. Turn oven off and DO NOT OPEN OVEN DOOR for 1½ hours. Cake will shrink from sides of pan and will not crack. Let cool completely before frosting. To make frosting, heat cream in the top of a double boiler. Add chocolate, stirring until melted and smooth. Let cool before spreading on cheesecake. When serving, slice in very thin pieces. This is a sinfully rich dessert.

Serves 15 to 20

Profiteroles with Banana Cream and Chocolate Sauce

Cream puffs with a difference!

Choux Pastry

1	cup water	250	mL
¼	cup butter	50	mL
1	cup all-purpose flour	250	mL
3-4	eggs, at room temperature	3-4	

Filling

⅔	cup whipped cream	150	mL
1	banana, mashed well	1	
	Juice of ½ lemon		
1	tablespoon brandy, to taste	15	mL

Chocolate Sauce

2	squares (each 1 oz/28 g) unsweetened chocolate	2	
6	tablespoons cold water	90-100	mL
¾	cup granulated sugar	175	mL
¼	teaspoon salt	1	mL
1	tablespoon butter	15	mL

Preheat oven to 350° F (180° C). Bring butter and water to a boil in a saucepan. Add flour all at once, stirring until dough comes away from the sides of the pan. Remove from heat; cool for 2 minutes. Add 1 egg at a time, beating well after each addition. Mixture should be thick enough to hold its shape. Drop from spoon in small profiterole shapes on a lightly greased baking sheet. Bake for 20 minutes, then prick pastry and return to oven for 5 to 10 minutes until dried. Remove and let cool.

To make filling, fold all filling ingredients together. For chocolate sauce, place chocolate and water in saucepan over low heat until chocolate melts and mixture becomes thick. Add sugar; stir until dissolved. Add salt and butter; stir to melt. Remove from heat. Profiteroles may be served warm or cold. To serve, break profiteroles open; fill with banana filling. The sauce may either be served as a puddle under the profiteroles or a drizzle over them.

Serves 6 to 8

Tiramisu

Decadent! Tiramisu literally means "pick-me-up" because of the extra-strong coffee used.

4	large eggs	4
6	tablespoons granulated sugar	100 mL
1	container (16 oz/450 g) mascarpone cheese	1
1	cup whipping cream, whipped	250 mL
2	cups extra-strong espresso	500 mL
¼-½	cup Kahlua or Marsala, more to taste	50-125 mL
1	package (8 oz/250 g) lady fingers (crispy Italian style) Cocoa (dark Dutch)	1

Beat eggs and sugar until light in color. Beat in mascarpone just until smooth. Fold whipped cream into egg-cheese mixture. Combine espresso and Kahlua in a small bowl. One at a time, quickly dip lady fingers completely in the mixture and then place side by side in an 11" x 7" (2 L) shallow dish. Break lady fingers, if necessary, to cover entire bottom. Cover with ½ of the egg-cheese mixture. Sprinkle evenly and solidly with cocoa. Add a second layer of dipped lady fingers; top with remaining cheese mixture. Sprinkle solidly with cocoa. Cover and refrigerate for several hours or overnight.

Serves 8 to 10

* This recipe requires very strong espresso in order to have the best flavor.

The Admiral's Favorite Dessert
You'll love it too!

1	can (10 oz/300 mL) Eagle Brand sweetened condensed milk	1
1½	cups crushed chocolate wafers	375 mL
⅓	cup butter, melted	75 mL
¼	cup granulated sugar	50 mL
3	bananas	3
½	cup whipping cream, whipped	125 mL
1	square (1 oz/28 g) semi-sweet chocolate	1

Place unopened can of condensed milk in a saucepan with enough water to completely cover. Gently simmer for 2½ to 3 hours, making sure the can remains covered with water at all times. Remove from pan and let cool. This process will produce delicious, creamy caramel.

Mix chocolate crumbs, butter and sugar in a 10" (25 cm) fluted quiche dish. Press mixture into dish with fingers to form a crust. Chill for 20 to 30 minutes in refrigerator. Open condensed milk can; spread cooled caramel over crust. Slice bananas; place on caramel to completely cover. Spread the whipped cream over the bananas; sealing completely so bananas will not darken. Garnish with chocolate curls. Refrigerate until serving time. May be made a day ahead as long as bananas are completely covered with whipped cream.

Serves 8 to 10

* The crust may be made with graham cracker crumbs or ginger crisp crumbs. A treat no matter how you slice it.

Ginger Snapped with Cream and Cointreau

1	box (7 oz/200 g) ginger snaps	1
2	cups whipping cream	500 mL
½	cup finely chopped candied ginger (found in bulk food stores)	125 mL
½	cup shredded coconut	125 mL
½	cup chopped walnuts	125 mL
¼	cup granulated sugar	50 mL
¼	cup Cointreau or Grand Marnier	50 mL

Break ginger snaps into quarters; set aside. Whip cream until stiff. Add remaining ingredients to whipped cream. Blend well. Layer cream mixture and ginger snaps in a large glass serving bowl until cream mixture is exhausted, making sure that the last layer is the cream mixture. Refrigerate until ready to serve.

Serves 10 or more

* In lieu of candied ginger, bottled stemmed ginger may be used.

Ginger Apricot Meringue

6	egg whites	6	
½	teaspoon cream of tartar	2	mL
1½	cups granulated sugar	375	mL
3	jars (each 4½ oz/128 mL) baby-food apricots	3	
1-2	tablespoons finely chopped crystallized ginger	15-25	mL
1	cup whipping cream, whipped	250	mL
½	cup sliced or slivered almonds, toasted	125	mL

Preheat oven to 275° F (140° C). Beat egg whites with cream of tartar until soft peaks form. Add sugar very gradually, beating well after each addition, until stiff glossy peaks form. Pencil two 8" (20 cm) circles on foil or brown paper; place on cookie sheet. Spread meringue smoothly over each circle. Bake for 45 minutes. Turn oven off. Leave meringue in the oven overnight with the door closed. Peel off foil. Place one meringue on a serving plate. Fold ginger into 2 jars of apricots; spread on first meringue. Top with second meringue. Fold remaining apricots into whipped cream. Spread over second meringue. Garnish with toasted almonds.

Serves 8

Orange Torte
This dessert looks terrific, tastes terrific and never fails!

1	cup graham cracker crumbs	250	mL
⅔	cup fresh orange juice	150	mL
6	egg yolks	6	
⅔	cup granulated sugar	150	mL
2	tablespoons grated orange rind	25	mL
1	cup ground almonds (preferably not blanched)	250	mL
6	egg whites	6	
¼	teaspoon salt	1	mL
⅔	cup granulated sugar	150	mL

Filling and topping

1	cup whipping cream	250	mL
	Grand Marnier to taste		

Garnish

Kiwifruit, strawberries or mandarin oranges
Toasted sliced almonds

Preheat oven to 350° F (180° C). Mix graham cracker crumbs with orange juice in a large bowl; set aside. Beat egg yolks with sugar until light and lemon-colored. In a separate bowl, mix orange rind with almonds; set aside. In another separate bowl, beat egg whites with salt until soft peaks form; gradually add sugar. Mix yolk mixture with crumb mixture; then gently add almond mixture. Carefully fold in egg whites. Pour into two 8" (1.2 L) round cake pans lined with waxed paper or cooking parchment. Bake in middle of oven for 30 minutes. Let cool on rack. To make filling, whip cream; flavor with Grand Marnier. Place one baked layer on a serving plate. Spread some filling on first layer; top with second baked layer. Spread remaining filling on top and sides of torte. Garnish top with drained mandarin orange sections, kiwifruit or strawberries; garnish the sides with toasted, sliced almonds. Refrigerate until serving time.

Serves 8

Orange Angel Cake Dessert

A very light dessert that can be made a day ahead.

2	cups cold fresh orange juice	500 mL
	Rind of 1 orange, grated	
	Rind of 1 lemon, grated	
1	cup granulated sugar	250 mL
1	envelope unflavored gelatin	1
	Juice of 1 lemon	
1	cup whipping cream	250 mL
1	small angel cake (or ⅔ of a large one)	1
1	can (10 oz/284 mL) mandarin oranges, drained	1
½	cup whole almonds, lightly toasted	125 mL

In a saucepan, combine ¾ cup (175 mL) of the orange juice, orange rind, lemon rind and sugar. Heat until sugar is dissolved. Soften gelatin in ¼ cup (50 mL) of the cold orange juice; add to hot mixture, stirring well. Remove from heat; add remaining 1 cup (250 mL) of cold orange juice and the lemon juice. Refrigerate until thick and syrupy, 2 to 3 hours. In a large bowl, whip cream. Fold orange mixture into whipped cream. Break cake into bite-sized pieces. In a glass serving dish, alternate layers of cake with orange mixture, ending with orange mixture. Garnish with mandarin oranges and almonds. Refrigerate until ready to serve.

Serves 8 to 10

Hazelnut Meringue with Fruit

A melt-in-your-mouth delicacy.

1	cup hazelnuts	250	mL
4	egg whites	4	
1	cup fruit sugar	250	mL
1	teaspoon white vinegar	5	mL
1	teaspoon vanilla	5	mL
2	cups whipping cream	500	mL
1	tablespoon granulated sugar	15	mL
½	teaspoon vanilla	2	mL
1	pint fresh raspberries or strawberries	500	mL
	Icing sugar		

Preheat oven to 325° F (160° C). Toast hazelnuts in the oven for 15 to 20 minutes. Remove from oven, place nuts in a tea towel and rub to remove skins. Chop finely; set aside. Beat egg whites until stiff. Add fruit sugar gradually. Add vinegar and vanilla; beat for 30 seconds. Fold in nuts. Line two 8" (1.2 L) round cake pans with parchment or brown paper. Spread meringue in prepared pans; bake for 30 to 40 minutes. Let stand in pans for 5 to 10 minutes, then turn out on racks to cool. Assemble 2 hours before serving. Whip cream; add sugar and vanilla. Place 1 meringue on a serving plate. Spread with whipped cream, then fruit. Top with second meringue; dust with icing sugar. Refrigerate until serving time.

Serves 8

* Serve this with Raspberry Cassis Coulis (see page 164) or with Strawberries Cardinal from *Fare for Friends*, page 159.

Pineapple Crunch

1	can (19 oz/540 mL) unsweetened, crushed pineapple	1
⅓	cup butter	75 mL
½	cup granulated sugar	125 mL
1	teaspoon vanilla	5 mL
1	egg	1
1¼	cups all-purpose flour, sifted	300 mL
1½	teaspoons baking powder	7 mL
¼	teaspoon salt	1 mL

Topping
½	cup coconut	125 mL
½	cup chopped walnuts	125 mL
⅓	cup brown sugar	75 mL
3	tablespoons butter, melted	50 mL

Preheat oven to 350° F (180° C). Drain pineapple, reserving ½ cup (125 mL) of the syrup. Cream butter, sugar and vanilla. Add egg; beat well. Sift flour, baking powder and salt together; add to creamed mixture alternately with pineapple syrup. Spread half of the mixture in greased and floured 9" (2.5 L) square cake pan. Spoon pineapple over this. Cover with remaining batter. Combine topping ingredients; sprinkle over batter. Bake for 35 to 40 minutes. Serve warm.

Serves 6 to 8

Apple-Walnut Cobbler
Best slightly warm from the oven, with cream or ice cream!

4	cups cooking apples (Cortland, Spy)	1	L
¼	cup granulated sugar	50	mL
½	teaspoon cinnamon	2	mL
1	cup all-purpose flour	250	mL
¾	cup granulated sugar	175	mL
1	teaspoon baking powder	5	mL
¼	teaspoon salt	1	mL
1	egg	1	
½	cup evaporated or homogenized milk	125	mL
⅓	cup melted butter	75	mL
¾	cup coarsely chopped walnuts	175	mL

Preheat oven to 325° F (160° C). Peel and slice apples thinly. Combine apples with the ¼ cup (50 mL) sugar and cinnamon; put into a 8" (2 L) square or round baking dish. Sift dry ingredients together. Blend egg, milk and butter. Add dry ingredients all at once to egg mixture; mix until smooth. Pour over apples. Sprinkle with walnuts. Bake for 50 to 55 minutes or until cake springs back when touched.

Serves 6 to 8

* May be served with pouring cream, whipped cream, ice cream or a slice of cheese.

Raisin Pudding

Just try to keep any leftovers!

Sauce

¾	cup brown sugar	175	mL
2½	cups water	625	mL
¼	cup butter	50	mL

Batter

¼	cup melted butter	50	mL
½	cup brown sugar	125	mL
½	cup milk	125	mL
1	teaspoon vanilla	5	mL
1	cup all-purpose flour	250	mL
	Pinch of salt		
2	teaspoons baking powder	10	mL
¾	cup raisins	175	mL
1	cup whipping cream, whipped	250	mL

Preheat oven to 350° F (180° C). In a saucepan, combine sauce ingredients. Heat until sugar is dissolved and butter melted. Pour into a large soufflé or casserole dish. In a bowl, combine butter, brown sugar, milk and vanilla. Add flour, salt and baking powder. Beat well. Stir in raisins. Spoon batter onto sauce. Bake for 40 minutes. Serve warm in bowls so you don't miss any of the sauce. Serve with whipped cream.

Serves 6 to 8

Bread and Butter Pudding

Old-fashioned comfort food.

3	tablespoons raisins	50	mL
3	tablespoons water	50	mL
1	cup milk	250	mL
1	cup whipping cream	250	mL
¼	teaspoon salt	1	mL
3	eggs	3	
½	cup granulated sugar	125	mL
1	teaspoon vanilla	5	mL
7	slices white bread	7	
2	tablespoons butter, softened	25	mL
2-3	tablespoons apricot jam	25-50	mL
	Icing sugar		

Preheat oven to 325° F (160° C). Soak raisins in water for at least 30 minutes. In a heavy saucepan, over low heat, combine milk, cream and salt. Heat slowly until hot but not boiling. In a large bowl, beat together eggs and sugar. Add vanilla. Slowly add milk mixture, stirring well. Butter bread; spread a very thin layer of apricot jam on top. Butter a shallow ovenproof dish; fit the bread snugly, in layers, cutting if necessary. Drain raisins; sprinkle over the bread layers. Pour custard over all. (Pudding can be left at room temperature for 1 to 2 hours at this stage.) Place dish in a pan of hot water; bake for 40 minutes. Crisp the surface under the broiler for 1 to 2 minutes. Remove from oven; sift icing sugar over the top. Serve warm.

Serves 6 to 8

Rhubarb and Apple Sponge

5	cups rhubarb, chopped	1.25	L
2	cooking apples, peeled, quartered and thinly sliced	2	
½	cup granulated sugar	125	mL
1	teaspoon grated lemon rind	5	mL
2	tablespoons water	25	mL
2	eggs	2	
⅓	cup granulated sugar	75	mL
2	tablespoons cornstarch	25	mL
¼	cup all-purpose flour	50	mL
½	teaspoon baking powder	2	mL

Preheat oven to 350° F (180° C). Combine rhubarb, apples, the ½ cup (125 mL) sugar, rind and water in a saucepan. Bring to a boil; lower heat and simmer, uncovered, for 15 minutes. Pour into a greased, deep, ovenproof dish. In a bowl, beat eggs until thick and creamy. Gradually add the ⅓ cup (75 mL) sugar, beating between additions, until dissolved. Mix cornstarch, flour and baking powder; fold into egg mixture. Spread over fruit; bake for 30 minutes. Serve warm or cold.

Serves 4 to 6

Drizzles and Puddles

These quick and easy little sauces can transform the simplest of fresh fruits into a grand presentation.

RASPBERRY CASSIS COULIS

1	package (10 oz/300 g) frozen unsweetened raspberries, thawed	1
1	tablespoon cassis	15 mL
1-3	tablespoons sugar, to taste	15-50 mL

Purée raspberries in food processor. Press through sieve to remove seeds. Stir in cassis and sugar.

Makes 1 cup (250 mL)

* Use as a sauce over fruit or as a puddle under fruit on a composed fruit dessert plate.

* Use fruits that contrast with the sauce (e.g., green grapes, honeydew, kiwifruit) for a striking visual effect.

* Use a spoonful of each of Raspberry Cassis Coulis and White-Chocolate Drizzle to make a two-toned puddle. Drag the tines of a fork through the two adjacent puddles to create a rainbow effect.

ORANGE-YOGURT SAUCE WITH GINGER

1	cup yogurt (no fat, low fat, your choice)	250 mL
1	tablespoon honey	15 mL
¼	cup orange marmalade	50 mL
1	tablespoon finely chopped crystallized ginger	15 mL

Combine all ingredients; chill until serving time.

Makes 1 cup (250 mL)

* May be used as a dip for a fruit tray.

BLUEBERRY GRAND MARNIER PURÉE

1	package (10 oz/300 g) frozen unsweetened blueberries, thawed	1
1	tablespoon Grand Marnier	15 mL
1	tablespoon granulated sugar	15 mL

Purée blueberries in food processor. Then rub through a sieve to remove skins. Stir in Grand Marnier and sugar.

Makes 1 cup (250 mL)

* Serve as a sauce over fruit or as a puddle under fruit on a composed fruit dessert plate. Garnish with lemon zest.

WHITE-CHOCOLATE DRIZZLE

¾	cup grated white chocolate	175 mL
3	tablespoons plain yogurt or whipping cream	50 mL

Melt chocolate in a double boiler over hot (but not boiling) water. Stir away unmelted pieces. Remove from heat; add yogurt. Stir.

Makes ½ cup (125 mL)

* Either drizzle sauce over fruit, cake or brownies, or make a puddle under fruit, etc., on serving plates.

* Use a spoonful of each of Raspberry Cassis Coulis and White-Chocolate Drizzle to make a two-toned puddle.

Peppered Strawberries

An incredible taste sensation – the pepper actually enhances the strawberry flavor!

6	cups strawberries	1.5 L
3	tablespoons sugar	50 mL
2	tablespoons kirsch or anisette	25 mL
2	tablespoons Grand Marnier	25 mL
	Freshly ground black pepper	
4	scoops strawberry ice cream	4
⅔	cup whipping cream, whipped	150 mL

Wash, hull and quarter strawberries. Mix them with sugar and liqueurs; marinate for 15 minutes. Dust mixture generously with black pepper, turning the grinder 25 times. Whisk strawberry ice cream until soft. Fold in whipped cream, then strawberries and marinade. Refrigerate until serving time. Serve in glass dishes.

Serves 6 to 8

Fresh Orange Slices in Marsala

Light, fresh, fast and delicious!

4	large oranges	4
½	cup orange juice	125 mL
1	tablespoon honey	15 mL
3	tablespoons Marsala	50 mL

Peel the oranges; remove all the pith. Slice as thinly as possible. Layer in a glass dish. Heat orange juice and honey until honey melts; add Marsala. Pour sauce over orange slices. Refrigerate for at least 3 to 4 hours or overnight.

Serves 4

Grand Marnier Fruit Dip

Fabulous!

1	cup Cool Whip	250	mL
1	package (8 oz/250 g) cream cheese	1	
¼	cup frozen orange juice concentrate	50	mL
2-4	tablespoons honey	25-50	mL
¼	cup Grand Marnier	50	mL
1	tablespoon orange zest	15	mL

Mix all ingredients together using a food processor or a mixer. Store in the refrigerator or in the freezer.

Makes 1½ to 2 cups (375 to 500 mL)

Lime Sublime

Light and fresh tasting – especially good with fruit.

4	egg yolks	4	
½	cup granulated sugar	125	mL
	Grated rind of 1 lime, orange or lemon		
¼	cup fresh lime, orange or lemon juice	50	mL
1	cup whipping cream	250	mL
	Fruit for garnish		

Beat together egg yolks, sugar, rind and juice for 5 minutes. Transfer to the top of a double boiler. Cook, stirring constantly until thick, about 10 minutes. Let cool. Whip cream until stiff; gently fold into egg-yolk mixture. Chill until serving time. Garnish with sliced kiwi, whole raspberries or the fruit of your choice.

Serves 4 to 6

Ice-Cream Peanut-Butter Pie

For your favorite child – 8 or 80!

1½	cups graham wafer crumbs	375	mL
⅓	cup brown sugar	75	mL
⅓	cup butter, melted	75	mL
⅓	cup crunchy peanut butter	75	mL
4	cups vanilla ice cream, softened	1	L
	Whipped cream for garnish		

In a large bowl, combine graham wafer crumbs, brown sugar, butter and peanut butter. Pat ½ of the crumbs in bottom of 9" (2.5 L) springform pan. Spread ice cream over crumbs. Sprinkle remaining crumbs on top; pat down lightly. Freeze until firm (at least 2 hours). Remove from freezer 10 minutes before serving. Pipe with whipped cream for garnish.

Serves 8 to 10

Avocado Ice Cream

An Australian taste sensation!

1	small carton (2 cups/500 mL) vanilla ice cream	1	
2	ripe avocados	2	
2	tablespoons honey	25	mL
2	tablespoons lemon or lime juice	25	mL
	Chopped pistachios and avocado to garnish		

Let ice cream soften at room temperature. Peel and pit avocados; mash avocados with honey and lemon juice. Quickly and thoroughly blend avocado mixture with ice cream; return to freezer for at least 4 hours. Soften slightly before serving. Serve in scoops garnished with chopped pistachios and avocado.

Serves 4 to 6

Frozen Lemon Fluff

This has the good flavor of lemon pie without the calories!

1	cup evaporated milk	250 mL
⅓	cup lemon juice	75 mL
2	eggs	2
¼	teaspoon salt	1 mL
½	cup granulated sugar	125 mL
1	tablespoon grated lemon rind	15 mL

Topping

1	cup cornflakes (uncrushed)	250 mL
3	tablespoons sugar	50 mL
2	tablespoons butter, melted	25 mL

Pour evaporated milk into a metal cake pan; freeze until ice crystals form around the edges. Scrape milk into a small chilled bowl; beat with electric beater at high speed until stiff, about 2 minutes. Add lemon juice; continue beating until very stiff. In larger bowl, beat eggs, salt and sugar at high speed until very thick and lemon-colored, about 5 minutes. Fold in whipped milk and lemon rind. Pour into a 10" (3 L) springform pan; place in freezer while preparing topping. Meanwhile, crush cornflakes in a bag or with a rolling pin. Combine with sugar and butter. Remove lemon mixture from freezer; sprinkle evenly with topping. Return to freezer; freeze until firm.

Serves 6 to 9

Orange-Lemon Ice

A light, refreshing 3-fruit ice – the perfect dessert to complement a filling entrée.

2	cups granulated sugar	500 mL
3	cups water	750 mL
	Juice of 3 oranges	
	Grated rind of 1 orange	
	Juice of 3 lemons	
	Grated rind of 1 lemon	
1	ripe banana, thoroughly mashed	1

In a large saucepan, combine sugar and water. Bring to a boil; simmer for 5 minutes. Remove from heat; stir in remaining ingredients. Pour into metal pan; freeze until it begins to set around the edges. Beat with a wire whisk or rotary beater. This should be repeated several times during the freezing process to break up the ice crystals and ensure a smooth finished product.

Makes 6 cups (1.5 L)

* Use an ice-cream scoop to serve on our Raspberry Cassis Coulis (see page 164) accompanied by Ginger Crisps (see page 187). Garnish with whole raspberries or mint leaves.

Cakes, Pies and Cookies

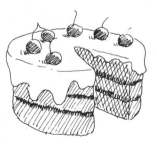

Chocolate, Chocolate, Chocolate Fudge Cake

A Chocoholic's Nirvana!

This cake has several different parts to be made, but none that has to be prepared at the last minute. The cake and syrup can be made the day before; the fudge filling and cream should be made the day you plan to serve the cake, but may be done early and refrigerated until assembly time. Enjoy!

Cake

⅔	cup unsalted butter at room temperature	150	mL
2	cups granulated sugar	500	mL
3	eggs	3	
2	cups all-purpose flour, sifted	500	mL
¾	cup Dutch dark cocoa	175	mL
1¼	teaspoons baking soda	6	mL
¼	teaspoon baking powder	1	mL
½	teaspoon salt	2	mL
1½	cups milk	375	mL
1	teaspoon vanilla	5	mL
¼	cup coffee liqueur	50	mL

Fudge filling

⅔	cup granulated sugar	150	mL
½	cup whipping cream	125	mL
2½	squares (each 1 oz/28 g) unsweetened chocolate	2½	
1	tablespoon light corn syrup	15	mL
2	tablespoons unsalted butter	25	mL

Chocolate Cream

2½	cups whipping cream	625	mL
4	tablespoons Dutch dark cocoa	50	mL
7	tablespoons icing sugar	100	mL

Chocolate Syrup

2	tablespoons Dutch dark cocoa	25	mL
2	tablespoons corn syrup	25	mL
1	tablespoon granulated sugar	15	mL
2	tablespoons water	25	mL

Preheat oven to 350° F (180° C). Grease and flour two 9" (1.5 L) round cake pans. Tap out excess flour; line bottoms with waxed paper. To make cake, in a large mixing bowl, beat butter until light and fluffy. Gradually add sugar and continue beating until smooth. Beat in eggs, one at a time, until well blended. Sift together the flour, cocoa, baking soda, baking powder and salt; add to egg mixture in thirds, alternately with milk, mixing each time just until blended. Stir in vanilla and liqueur. Divide batter evenly between pans; bake for 40 to 45 minutes or until springy. Let cool for 30 minutes on a wire rack. Loosen edges and unmold; peel off paper. Let cool completely on rack. If making a day in advance, wrap cake layers well after cooling.

To make fudge filling, combine sugar, cream, chocolate and corn syrup in a small, heavy saucepan. Bring to a simmer over moderate heat, stirring frequently. Reduce heat to low and cook for about 10 minutes until mixture thickens. Remove from heat, dot top with butter and let cool to room temperature (about 15 minutes). Stir in butter until smooth and creamy. Set aside.

For chocolate cream, combine cream and cocoa; chill together in refrigerator for at least 1 hour. Beat until it holds soft peaks; gradually add sugar, beating until stiff.

To make chocolate syrup, combine all syrup ingredients in a small saucepan. Bring to a simmer over low heat; cook, stirring constantly, for about 2 minutes. Transfer to a small bowl; let cool to room temperature, stirring once or twice to prevent a skin from forming. (This can be made a day in advance.) About 3 hours before serving, place one cake layer on a beautiful plate; cover with all of the fudge filling. Spread approximately 1 cup (250 mL) of the chocolate cream over the fudge filling. Cover with the second cake layer. Frost top and sides with remaining chocolate cream. Refrigerate. Just before serving, drizzle the syrup over the top in a lacy pattern. You may not need all of the syrup.

Serves 12 to 16

* Garnish with large chocolate curls if you feel like gilding the lily!

Orange Rum Cake

A delicious cake that needs to be baked a day or two before serving, and stays fresh for a week.

1	cup butter or margarine	250	mL
1	cup granulated sugar	250	mL
	Grated rind of 2 large oranges		
	Grated rind of 1 lemon		
2	eggs	2	
2½	cups sifted all-purpose flour	625	mL
2	tablespoons baking powder	25	mL
1	teaspoon baking soda	5	mL
½	teaspoon salt	2	mL
1	cup buttermilk	250	mL
1	cup finely chopped walnuts	250	mL

Glaze

	Juice of 2 large oranges		
	Juice of 1 lemon		
⅔	cup sugar	150	mL
2	tablespoons rum	25	mL
	Walnut halves		

Preheat oven to 350° F (180° C). Beat butter in large bowl until fluffy. Gradually add sugar, beating after each addition. Add orange and lemon rind. Add eggs, one at a time, beating after each addition until very light. Sift flour, baking powder, baking soda and salt. Add dry ingredients to the butter mixture alternately with buttermilk, beating well after each addition. Fold in chopped walnuts; pour batter into greased 9" (3 L) or 10" (4 L) tube pan. Bake for 50 minutes or until the cake is done (when it shrinks from side of pan and springs back when lightly touched). Remove from oven. Do not remove cake from pan.

To make glaze, strain orange and lemon juice into saucepan; add sugar and rum. Bring to a boil. Pour slowly over cake in tube pan. Let cool for 30 minutes before turning out on rack. Garnish with walnut halves. Let cake stand a day or two before serving. (It can be frozen.)

Serves 10

* 1 cup (250 mL) buttermilk can be replaced with ½ cup (125 mL) milk mixed with ½ cup (125 mL) yogurt.

Orange Take-Along Cake

You'll love this moist delicious cake.

1¼	cups boiling water	300	mL
1	cup quick-cooking oats	250	mL
½	cup butter, softened	125	mL
1	cup granulated sugar	250	mL
½	cup packed brown sugar	125	mL
2	eggs	2	
¼	cup frozen orange juice concentrate	50	mL
1	teaspoon vanilla	5	mL
1¾	cups all-purpose flour	425	mL
1	teaspoon baking powder	5	mL
1	teaspoon baking soda	5	mL
½	teaspoon salt	2	mL
½	teaspoon ground cinnamon	2	mL
½	cup chopped pecans or walnuts	125	mL

Double-Nut Topping

½	cup packed brown sugar	125	mL
¼	cup butter	50	mL
2	tablespoons frozen orange juice concentrate	25	mL
1	cup flaked coconut	250	mL
½	cup chopped pecans or walnuts	125	mL

Preheat oven to 350° F (180° C). Grease and flour a 13" x 9" (3.5 L) cake pan. Pour boiling water over oats; set aside. Cream butter with sugars. Beat in eggs one at a time. Beat in the ¼ cup (50 mL) orange juice concentrate and vanilla. Sift flour together with baking powder, baking soda, salt and cinnamon; blend flour mixture into creamed mixture alternately with oat mixture, beginning and ending with flour mixture. Fold in nuts. Spoon into prepared pan. Bake for 40 minutes; remove from oven. Let cool.

To make topping, combine sugar, butter and orange juice concentrate in a saucepan; boil for 1 minute. Stir in coconut and pecans. Spread on cooled cake; broil until brown and bubbly. Be careful not to burn.

Serves 12 to 15

Pineapple Fruitcake

Great for the festive season.

¾	cup butter	175	mL
⅔	cup granulated sugar	150	mL
2	eggs	2	
1	can (19 oz/540 mL) crushed pineapple (undrained)	1	
1	pound sultana raisins, plumped in hot water, then drained and dried	500	g
½	pound whole candied cherries	250	g
¼	pound candied mixed peel or candied mixed fruit	125	g
1	cup coconut (optional)	250	mL
3	cups all-purpose flour, sifted	750	mL
1	tablespoon baking powder	15	mL
½	teaspoon salt	2	mL

Preheat oven to 300° F (150° C). Grease two 8" x 4" (1.5 L) loaf pans. Line pans, first with brown paper, then with 2 layers of waxed paper. In a large bowl, cream butter and sugar well. Add eggs, one at a time, beating after each addition. Stir in pineapple. Mix raisins, cherries, peel and coconut (if using) together; toss with 1 cup (250 mL) of the flour until fruit is coated. Sift together the remaining 2 cups (500 mL) flour with the baking powder and salt. Stir flour mixture and fruit mixture into the batter. Divide in two loaf pans. Bake for 1½ hours. Do not overbake. A metal skewer inserted in the center of loaf will come out clean when loaf is baked. Keep refrigerated.

Makes 2 loaves

* A pan of water on a lower oven shelf will keep the cake moist.

Applesauce Loaf Cake

½	cup butter, softened	125	mL
¾	cup granulated sugar	175	mL
1	cup unsweetened applesauce	250	mL
2	cups cake-and-pastry flour	500	mL
1	teaspoon baking soda	5	mL
½	teaspoon salt	2	mL
¼	teaspoon ground nutmeg	1	mL
¼	teaspoon ground cinnamon	1	mL
1	teaspoon lemon juice	5	mL
1	cup raisins	250	mL
½	cup chopped walnuts	125	mL

Preheat oven to 350° F (180° C). Grease and flour a 9" x 5" (2 L) loaf pan. Cream butter and sugar. Add applesauce. Sift flour with baking soda, salt and spices; add to applesauce mixture. Add lemon juice; mix well. Stir in raisins and walnuts. Pour into pan; bake for 50 minutes or until toothpick inserted comes out clean.

Serves 10 to 12

Surprise Cupcakes
Special birthday-party cupcakes – one for every classmate!

Filling

1	package (8 oz/250 g) cream cheese, softened	1	
1	egg	1	
⅓	cup granulated sugar	75	mL
½	teaspoon salt	2	mL
¾	cup chocolate chips	175	mL

Batter

3	cups all-purpose flour	750	mL
2	cups granulated sugar	500	mL
½	cup cocoa	125	mL
1	teaspoon salt	5	mL
2	teaspoons baking soda	10	mL
2	cups water	500	mL
⅔	cup vegetable oil	150	mL
2	tablespoons white vinegar	25	mL
2	teaspoons vanilla	10	mL

Preheat oven to 350° F (180° C). To make filling, combine cream cheese, egg, sugar and salt. Beat until smooth. Stir in chocolate chips; set aside.

To make batter, sift dry ingredients into a large mixing bowl. Add wet ingredients; beat until smooth. Grease muffin tins or line with paper baking cups. Fill pans ⅔ full with batter. Top each with a generous teaspoon of filling. Bake for 25 minutes. May be frozen.

Makes 2½ dozen

Plum Pie

Definitely delicious!

6	cups prune plums (unpeeled), pitted and cut in thick slices	1.5	L
1	tablespoon grated orange rind	15	mL
2	tablespoons orange juice	25	mL
⅔	cup granulated sugar	150	mL
3	tablespoons all-purpose flour	50	mL
½	teaspoon ground cinnamon	2	mL
¼	teaspoon ground nutmeg	1	mL
	Pastry for a 10" (25 cm) double-crust pie		

Preheat oven to 425° F (220° C). In a large bowl, combine all ingredients except pastry. Let stand for 10 minutes. Roll out bottom pastry; fit into 10" (25 cm) pie plate. Place fruit in pastry-lined pie plate; top with second crust or a lattice top. Seal edges; cut a vent in the top to allow steam to escape. Bake for 15 minutes; lower the oven temperature to 375° F (190° C) and continue baking for 30 minutes or until bubbly.

Serves 8

* Serve with ice cream or whipped cream.

* For a casual "country look," roll one crust about 2" (5 cm) larger than the pie plate. Fill crust with fruit, draw the excess pastry up and fold over fruit, leaving the center open.

Berry Crisp Pie

Yummy combination of fruit.

1	deep 10" (25 cm) pie shell (unbaked)	1

Crisp Topping

⅔	cup packed brown sugar	150	mL
½	cup all-purpose flour	125	mL
⅓	cup rolled oats	75	mL
⅓	cup butter	75	mL

Filling

3	cups frozen unsweetened blueberries	750	mL
2	cups frozen unsweetened raspberries	500	mL
1	cup frozen unsweetened strawberries	250	mL
⅔	cup granulated sugar	150	mL
3	tablespoons quick-cooking tapioca	50	mL
¼	teaspoon ground nutmeg	1	mL

Preheat oven to 425° F (220° C). Do not thaw fruit. For the topping, combine sugar, flour and rolled oats. Cut in butter until crumbly; set aside.

In a large bowl, combine frozen berries. In a small bowl, stir together sugar, tapicoa and nutmeg. Sprinkle over berries, tossing to coat evenly. Spoon into pie shell. Sprinkle topping over fruit. Bake for 15 minutes. Reduce heat to 350° F (180° C); continue baking for 1 hour or until the pastry is golden, the topping is brown and crisp, and the filling is bubbly. Let cool on rack.

Serves 8

* This is also delicious without the pastry, and served as a "berry crisp."

Pumpkin Crunch Pie

1	10" (25 cm) pie shell (unbaked)	1	
	Egg white, lightly beaten		
1½	cups pumpkin purée	375	mL
⅔	cup granulated sugar	150	mL
½	teaspoon salt	2	mL
1	teaspoon ground ginger	5	mL
1¼	teaspoons ground cinnamon	6	mL
½	teaspoon ground nutmeg	2	mL
¼	teaspoon cloves	1	mL
¼	teaspoon mace	1	mL
1	tablespoon molasses	15	mL
1	teaspoon grated orange rind	5	mL
4	teaspoons rum	20	mL
3	eggs, lightly beaten	3	
1¼	cups milk	300	mL
¾	cup evaporated milk	175	mL

Crunch Topping

1	tablespoon butter, softened	15	mL
1	tablespoon brown sugar	15	mL
1	teaspoon grated orange rind	5	mL
½	cup chopped walnuts or pecans	125	mL

Heat oven to 450° F (230° C). Brush pie shell with a little egg white to prevent crust from becoming soggy. Combine pumpkin, sugar, salt, spices, molasses, orange rind and rum. Add eggs, milk and evaporated milk. Blend. Pour into shell. Bake on bottom shelf of oven for 10 minutes; reduce heat to 325° F (160° C). Continue baking for about 45 minutes or until filling does not adhere to a knife.

Meanwhile, to make crunch topping, combine butter, sugar, orange rind and nuts. Sprinkle mixture over cooked pie; bake until nuts are slightly brown, about 5 minutes.

Serves 8

* Serve with whipped cream, if desired.

Apple-Lemon Pie
Apple pie with a new twist.

6	tablespoons butter or margarine, softened	90	mL
6	tablespoons granulated sugar	90	mL
2	eggs	2	
4	large apples, peeled and coarsely grated	4	
	Juice of 1 to 1½ lemons		
1	9" (23 cm) pie shell (unbaked)	1	
	Whipped cream or ice cream		

Preheat oven to 425° F (220° C). Cream butter and sugar well. Mix in eggs, one at a time. Stir in apples, then lemon juice. Fill pie shell; bake for 20 minutes. Reduce heat to 350° F (180° C); continue baking for 25 minutes. Serve with whipped cream.

Serves 6 to 8

Butter Tarts

1	egg, beaten	1	
⅔	cup brown sugar	150	mL
⅓	cup corn syrup	75	mL
¼	cup butter	50	mL
¾	cup raisins or currants	175	mL
¼	cup chopped walnuts or pecans	50	mL
¾	teaspoon vanilla	4	mL
	Pinch of salt		
12	large tart shells (unbaked)	12	

Preheat oven to 375° F (190° C). Combine egg, brown sugar and corn syrup. Cut in butter, leaving pea-sized pieces. Add raisins, walnuts, vanilla and salt. Spoon into tart shells so they are no more than ½ to ¾ full. Bake in oven for 20 to 25 minutes. If the tarts start to boil over, turn the heat down to 350° F (180° C).

Makes 12 large tarts

Maple Pecan Squares

Crust

1¼	cups all-purpose flour	300	mL
¼	cup brown sugar	50	mL
½	cup melted butter	125	mL

Topping

⅔	cup brown sugar	150	mL
¾	cup maple syrup	175	mL
¼	cup butter	50	mL
¼	teaspoon salt (optional)	1	mL
1	cup pecan halves	250	mL
½	teaspoon vanilla	2	mL
2	tablespoons all-purpose flour	25	mL
2	eggs, beaten	2	

Preheat oven to 350° F (180° C). For crust, mix flour, sugar and butter; press into an 11" x 7" (2 L) baking pan. Bake for 5 minutes. Remove from oven. Increase oven heat to 450° F (230° C).

To make the topping, simmer sugar and syrup for 5 minutes. Mix in the rest of the ingredients; pour over base. Bake for 10 minutes; reduce heat to 350° F (180° C) and bake for 20 minutes. Cut squares when cool. Store in airtight container.

Makes approximately 2 dozen

Turtle Squares
Truly decadent!

1	cup all-purpose flour	250	mL
½	cup brown sugar	125	mL
¼	cup unsalted butter	50	mL
½	cup pecan halves	125	mL
⅓	cup unsalted butter	75	mL
¼	cup brown sugar	50	mL
	Pinch of salt		
½	cup semi-sweet chocolate chips	125	mL

Preheat oven to 350° F (180° C). Place flour, sugar and the ¼ cup (50 mL) butter in food processor; blend until fine. Pat evenly into ungreased 8" (2 L) square pan. Sprinkle pecans on top. Mix remaining butter, sugar and salt in saucepan; bring to a boil for 10 to 20 seconds. Stir to mix. Pour evenly over nuts and crust. Bake for 18 to 20 minutes, until bubbly. Remove from oven. Sprinkle with chocolate chips. When melted, swirl chocolate with a knife or fork. Cut when cool. Store in airtight container.

Makes approximately 2½ dozen

Sticky 'n' Gooey but Good Bars

1	cup all-purpose flour, sifted	250	mL
½	teaspoon baking soda	2	mL
1	cup quick-cooking rolled oats	250	mL
	(see note below)		
¾	cup brown sugar	175	mL
½	cup butter, melted	125	mL
1	cup semi-sweet chocolate chips	250	mL
½	cup chopped nuts	125	mL
24	vanilla caramels	24	
1	cup whipping cream	250	mL

Preheat oven to 350° F (180° C). Combine flour, baking soda, rolled oats, brown sugar and melted butter. Mix well. Press ½ of this mixture into a 13" x 9" (3.5 L) baking pan. Bake for 8 minutes. Sprinkle with chocolate chips and nuts. Melt caramels with cream over low heat, stirring occasionally; pour over chips and nuts. Sprinkle remaining oat mixture over top. Bake for 20 minutes.

Makes 3 to 4 dozen.

* If you substitute large-flake rolled oats, chop by hand or in a food processor until texture of quick-cooking oats.

Almond-Crisp Cookies

Attractive served in a basket.

½	cup butter	125 mL
¾	cup granulated sugar	175 mL
2	egg whites	2
1	cup all-purpose flour	250 mL
1¼	cups sliced almonds	300 mL

Preheat oven to 300° F (150° C). Cream together butter and sugar. Add egg whites; beat until smooth. Stir in flour. Spread paper thin and right to the edges on 2 large, well-greased cookie sheets. Sprinkle almonds on top. Bake for 25 minutes, watching very carefully. Almonds should be pale brown. Remove from oven and let cool. Break into pieces.

Makes a generous quantity

Chocolate Crispie Balls

Always the first to disappear from a cookie tray.

½	cup butter or margarine, softened	125 mL
¾	cup peanut butter	175 mL
2	cups icing sugar	500 mL
½	teaspoon vanilla	2 mL
1¾	cups Rice Krispies	425 mL
1¼	cups semi-sweet chocolate chips	300 mL
4	teaspoons paraffin wax	20 mL

In a large mixing bowl, cream together butter and peanut butter. Stir in icing sugar and vanilla. Mix well. Stir in Rice Krispies. If mixture is too stiff, add a little more butter or margarine. Shape into 1" (2.5 cm) balls. Chill for 1 hour. Melt chocolate chips and paraffin in a round-bottomed bowl over hot water. Using two skewers, roll the chilled balls in the chocolate to coat. Lift the dipped balls out; set on waxed paper until firm. Store in refrigerator.

Makes 48 to 60

Ginger Crisps

¾	cup butter, softened	175	mL
1	cup granulated sugar	250	mL
1	egg	1	
¼	cup molasses	50	mL
1	teaspoon baking soda	5	mL
1	teaspoon ground ginger	5	mL
1	teaspoon ground cinnamon	5	mL
1	teaspoon ground cloves	5	mL
2	cups all-purpose flour	500	mL

Preheat oven to 400° F (200° C). In a mixing bowl, cream butter and sugar. Beat in egg, then molasses. Sift together baking soda, spices and flour. Stir into butter mixture, mixing until well blended. Roll dough into small balls; place on cookie sheets. Flatten with a fork dipped in sugar. Bake for 7 to 8 minutes. Remove from cookie sheet while still warm; let cool on a wire rack. These keep well in an airtight container.

Makes 4 dozen

Peanut and Cornflake Macaroons

2	egg whites	2	
½	cup granulated sugar	125	mL
1	teaspoon vanilla	5	mL
1	cup peanuts	250	mL
2	cups cornflakes	500	mL

Preheat oven to 325° F (160° C). Beat egg whites until stiff. Continue beating while gradually adding sugar. Add vanilla. Stir in peanuts and cornflakes. Drop by teaspoonfuls onto greased baking sheet. Bake for 10 to 15 minutes. Parchment paper may be used on baking sheet if desired.

Makes 3 dozen

Lauren's Crunch Bar Cookies

SKOR a hit with these cookies.

¾	cup white chocolate (5 oz./140 g)	175	mL
½	cup brown sugar	125	mL
½	cup granulated sugar	125	mL
¼	cup corn syrup	50	mL
1	egg	1	
½	cup melted butter	125	mL
2	teaspoons vanilla	10	mL
1½-2	cups all-purpose flour	375-500	mL
½	teaspoon baking soda	2	mL
½	teaspoon salt	2	mL
¾	cup semi-sweet chocolate chips	175	mL
¾	cup chopped nuts	175	mL
3	SKOR chocolate bars, broken	3	

Preheat oven to 350° F (180° C). In a food processor, grind white chocolate into fine chunks (or chop by hand). Add sugars; continue to blend. Gradually pour in syrup, egg, melted butter and vanilla. Transfer to a large mixing bowl. In a separate bowl, mix together flour, baking soda and salt. Stir the flour mixture into the batter. Add chocolate chips and nuts. Mix thoroughly. Drop batter in teaspoonfuls, 2" (5 cm) apart, onto a greased baking sheet. Press a small broken piece of SKOR chocolate bar into center of each cookie. Bake for 11 to 12 minutes. Let cool slightly on baking sheet before removing. Store in airtight container.

Makes 24 to 36

Jam Diagonals
Colorful addition to a festive cookie tray.

1	cup butter, softened	250	mL
½	cup granulated sugar	125	mL
2	teaspoons vanilla	10	mL
¼	teaspoon salt	1	mL
2-2½	cups all-purpose flour	500-625	mL
½	cup seedless raspberry jam or apricot jam	125	mL

Icing

½	cup icing sugar	125	mL
1	tablespoon lemon juice	15	mL

Preheat oven to 350° F (180° C). Cream butter, sugar, vanilla and salt until fluffy. Gradually stir in flour. Divide dough into 6 even portions. On lightly floured surface, using hands, roll each portion into a 9" (23 cm) rope. Flatten slightly. Place ropes 1" (2.5 cm) apart on a greased cookie sheet. With finger, make a depression, ½" (1.25 cm) wide, all the way down the center of each rope. Fill depression with jam. Bake for 12 to 15 minutes. Let cool completely (at least 1 hour) on cookie sheet, as cookie strips are very fragile while warm.

For icing, blend icing sugar with lemon juice until smooth. Drizzle over COOLED cookies while still on cookie sheet. When icing has set, cut diagonally into 1" (2.5 cm) cookies. These cookies freeze beautifully while still in strips. Freeze first on cookie sheet and then wrap. Slice just before serving.

Makes 4 dozen

Oat Cakes

An adult cookie – not too sweet.

¼	teaspoon baking soda	1	mL
⅓	cup boiling water	75	mL
⅔	cup granulated sugar	150	mL
1	cup large-flake rolled oats	250	mL
1	cup all-purpose flour	250	mL
1	cup bran	250	mL
½	teaspoon baking powder	2	mL
½	cup margarine or butter	125	mL

Preheat oven to 400° F (200° C). Dissolve baking soda in boiling water; set aside. In a separate bowl, combine sugar, oats, flour, bran and baking powder. Cut in margarine. Stir in water and baking soda until dough is evenly moistened. Form into two balls. Roll out on lightly floured surface to ⅛" to ¼" (3 mm to 5 mm) thick. Cut into 2" (5 cm) squares or triangles. Place on a lightly greased cookie sheet. Bake for 8 to 10 minutes or until slightly browned. Serve warm or at room temperature.

Makes about 36

Condiments

Roasted Red Pepper Sauce

So many uses!

2-3	sweet red peppers	2-3	
½	cup chopped onion	125	mL
1	clove garlic, chopped	1	
4	teaspoons olive oil	20	mL
¼	teaspoon salt	1	mL
	Pinch of pepper		
1½	teaspoons balsamic vinegar	7	mL
1	teaspoon lemon juice	5	mL
½	teaspoon seeded and chopped jalapeño pepper (optional)	2	mL

Preheat oven to 500° F (260° C). Place whole red peppers on a foil-lined baking pan; pierce skin with fork. Roast until skin is black. Remove from oven; let cool. Peel and discard stem and seeds. Purée the remaining flesh in food processor or blender. Sauté onions and garlic in hot olive oil until soft but not brown. Add onion mixture (including oil) to the purée; process until smooth. Add salt, pepper, vinegar and lemon juice. Stir in finely chopped jalapeño peppers (if using). Serve at room temperature. Makes about 1 cup (250 mL)

* Serve with roasted pork tenderloin, steak or fish.

VARIATIONS

*Dressing for Chicken Salad or Cold Chicken Slices

¼	cup roasted red pepper purée	50	mL
¼	cup plain yogurt	50	mL
1	tablespoon mayonnaise	15	mL

Mix purée, yogurt and mayonnaise together. Use as an accompaniment to sliced cold chicken or to bind chunks of chicken in a salad with chopped green onion.

*Vinaigrette for Cold Asparagus, Green Beans or Tossed Greens

1	tablespoon red pepper purée	15	mL
1	tablespoon red wine or balsamic vinegar	15	mL
3	tablespoons olive oil	50	mL
	Pinch of salt and pepper		

Put all ingredients in a jar and shake well to mix. Serve with cold cooked asparagus, green beans or with salad greens. This dressing separates easily, so add to salad just before serving.

Creamy Horseradish Sauce with Apple

¼	cup horseradish, drained and pressed dry	50 mL
3	tablespoons mayonnaise	50 mL
1	tablespoon cider vinegar	15 mL
1	tablespoon grainy Dijon mustard	15 mL
½	teaspoon crushed tarragon	2 mL
1½	teaspoons granulated sugar	7 mL
¼	teaspoon salt	1 mL
	Dash hot pepper sauce	
¼	cup unpeeled and grated tart apple	50 mL
3	tablespoons finely chopped red onion	50 mL

Mix all ingredients except apple and onion; then, fold in apple and onion. Store in refrigerator for several hours to blend flavors.

Makes about 1 cup (250 mL)

Sassy Sauce

A savory condiment with countless uses.

½	cup prepared horseradish	125 mL
½	cup Dijon mustard	125 mL
¼	cup liquid honey	50 mL
3	tablespoons dried minced onion	50 mL
1	teaspoon Beau Monde or celery salt	5 mL

Whisk all ingredients together until well mixed. (Place in a container with a tight lid; store in the refrigerator. Will keep for up to 2 months.)

Makes about 1½ cups (375 mL)

* Use a dollop of this in your favorite vinaigrette, as a substitute for Dijon mustard or horseradish, and as a condiment or glaze for beef, lamb, ham or chicken.

* Small jars of Sassy Sauce make a welcome gift.

Cumberland Sauce

Great served with pâté and crackers, or as a condiment with any type of game.

1	cup red currant jelly	250	mL
1	cup Port wine	250	mL
	Zest of 1 orange		
	Zest of 1 lemon		
3	tablespoons orange juice	50	mL
3	tablespoons lemon juice	50	mL
2	teaspoons hot English mustard	10	mL
¼	teaspoon ground ginger	1	mL
	Pinch of cayenne pepper		
2	tablespoons very finely chopped green onion	25	mL

In saucepan, melt red currant jelly slowly over low heat. Add wine, orange zest, lemon zest, orange juice and lemon juice. Stir in mustard (if you use dry mustard, make into paste first); add ginger and cayenne pepper. Boil for about 15 minutes. Stir in green onions. Let cool; then refrigerate until serving time. Keeps well. Make sauce a few days before serving to allow flavors to blend.

Makes about 2 cups (500 mL)

Spiced Peaches

Delicious with ham, pork or chicken.

1	can (28 oz/796 mL) sliced peaches	1
½	cup white vinegar	125 mL
⅔	cup brown sugar	150 mL
12	whole cloves	12
1	4" (10 cm) stick cinnamon	1

Drain syrup from peaches into a saucepan. Set peaches aside. Add remaining ingredients to syrup; bring to a boil. Lower heat; simmer for 10 minutes. Add peaches; simmer for 2 minutes. Let stand for a few hours for flavors to develop. Serve hot or cold. Keeps well in refrigerator for about a week.

Makes about 2 cups (500 mL)

Spiced Pineapple

1	can (19 oz/540 mL) pineapple chunks	1
½	cup white vinegar	125 mL
⅔	cup granulated sugar	150 mL
6-8	whole cloves	6-8
1	4" (10 cm) stick cinnamon	1

Drain pineapple, reserving fruit and juice. Add vinegar, sugar, cloves and cinnamon to reserved juice. Bring liquid to a boil. Reduce heat; simmer for 10 minutes. Add pineapple; bring to a boil. Remove from heat; refrigerate. Drain just before serving.

Makes about 1½ cups (375 mL)

* Serve with ham or on a toothpick as an hors d'oeuvre.

Spiced Grapes

Serve as a savory sauce with hot or cold meats.

5	pounds Concord grapes	2.5	kg
2	cups cider vinegar	500	mL
8	cups granulated sugar	2	L
1	tablespoon allspice	15	mL
1	tablespoon ground cloves	15	mL
1	tablespoon ground cinnamon	15	mL
½	teaspoon mace	2	mL

Squeeze grape pulp out of skins into a saucepan. Retain skins. Cook pulp over medium heat for 5 to 8 minutes to loosen seeds. Place pulp in a coarse sieve; press through to remove seeds. Discard seeds and retain pulp. Make syrup by dissolving sugar in hot vinegar; then add spices. Add skins and pulp; cook for 30 minutes or until thickened. Place in hot, sterilized jars; seal with paraffin wax or self-sealing lids.

Makes 8 jars (each 8 oz/250 mL)

Tomato Butter
Begin making this the night before.

6	quarts fully ripe tomatoes, peeled and chopped	6	L
3	cups granulated sugar	750	mL
5½	cups (1 kg bag) brown sugar	1.4	L
½	hot red pepper, chopped	½	
1	teaspoon ground cloves	5	mL
1¼	teaspoons allspice	6	mL
1	tablespoon ground cinnamon	15	mL
1	tablespoon salt	15	mL

Place tomatoes in a large colander; let drain, covered, overnight. In the morning, press the tomatoes a little to drain away excess liquid. Place tomatoes in large preserving kettle; add remaining ingredients. Bring to a full boil. Reduce heat; cook gently for about 2 hours, uncovered, stirring occasionally to prevent sticking. Adjust seasonings; cook for 30 minutes or until sauce thickens.

Makes approximately 10 jars (each 8 oz /250 mL)

* Try mixing some of this with hot salsa when making Tex-Mex Taco Dip (see page 11).

Susan's Sun-Dried Tomatoes

Oven-dried ... perfect results.

Plum tomatoes (any quantity)

Preheat oven to 225° F (110° C). Wash and dry tomatoes. Cut in half lengthwise (very large tomatoes should be quartered lengthwise). Spread tomatoes on cookie sheets, cut side up. Bake for 10 to 12 hours; remove from oven when dry and prune-like but still pliable. Watch carefully during the last hour or 2 of cooking, as tomatoes can go from being perfect to being scorched quickly. Let cool. Store either in plastic bags in the freezer or in jars covered with olive oil. Oil may be flavored with a clove of garlic and a few basil leaves, if desired.

Makes any quantity you like

Quick Lime Mayonnaise

Serve with fish or salads.

2	egg yolks	2	
½	teaspoon salt	2	mL
1	teaspoon hot English mustard	5	mL
¼	teaspoon Worcestershire sauce	1	mL
3	tablespoons fresh lime juice	50	mL
1	cup oil (vegetable and sunflower or all sunflower)	250	mL

Place first 5 ingredients in a blender or food processor. Cover and process at low speed to blend. Remove cover. With the motor running, add oil in a thin stream and blend until thick and smooth. Cover and store in refrigerator.

Makes 1½ cups (375 mL)

Perfect Pimiento

The best pimiento you have ever eaten!!

Sweet red or green peppers
Olive oil
Garlic cloves

Brine

½	cup coarse pickling salt	125	mL
8	quarts cold water	8	L

Syrup

1	cup vinegar	250	mL
1	cup granulated sugar	250	mL
3	cups water	750	mL

Halve and remove seeds and stems of peppers. In a large non-aluminum pot, mix brine until salt dissolves. Add seeded pepper halves; let stand in refrigerator overnight. In the morning, drain brine from peppers. Make syrup by boiling together vinegar, sugar and water. (You may have to make another batch of syrup if you have a lot of peppers.) Keep syrup simmering. In a saucepan, place enough peppers to fill two jars. Cover with cold water and bring to a rolling boil. Remove pan immediately from the heat; drain. Pack peppers in hot sterilized jars. Add 1 clove of garlic and 1 teaspoon (5 mL) olive oil to each jar. Cover with boiling syrup; seal with self-sealing lids. Repeat, using fresh cold water for each 2-jar lot of peppers. Store in cool place.

Makes as much as you like

* Use as garnish or in egg salad, casseroles, cabbage salad, sandwich fillings and bean salad.

Mother's Red and Green Tomato Chow Chow

Old-fashioned Maritime relish – good with meats and fish.

3	baskets (each 4 qt/4 L) red or green tomatoes (approximately 60)	3
5	pounds onions (approximately 20), coarsely chopped	2.5 kg
½	cup pickling salt	125 mL
1	quart cider vinegar	1 L
½	teaspoon cloves	2 mL
½	teaspoon mixed pickling spices	2 mL
½	teaspoon allspice	2 mL
4 +	sticks of cinnamon, broken	4 +
1	teaspoon dry mustard	5 mL
	Pinch of cayenne	
3	cups granulated sugar	750 mL

To prepare tomatoes, remove stem area, but do not peel. Chop in chunks; combine with onions in a large pickling kettle. Cover with salt; let stand overnight. Drain off liquid. In a large bowl, stir together 1 cup (250 mL) of the vinegar and remaining ingredients, stirring until dissolved. Add remaining vinegar; pour over vegetables. Boil gently for 2 hours or more, stirring from time to time so it does not stick. Mixture should become quite thick. Ladle into hot sterilized jars with self-sealing lids. Store in a cool dark place.

Makes 24 cups (6 L)

Bread and Butter Pickles

Crunchy in that ham sandwich!

4	quarts cucumbers (1"/2.5 cm in diameter)	4	L
2	sweet green peppers, cut in julienne strips	2	
1	sweet red pepper, cut in julienne strips	1	
8	white onions, sliced thinly	8	
½	cup pickling salt	125	mL
	Ice cubes		
5	cups white vinegar	1.25	L
5	cups granulated sugar	1.25	L
1	teaspoon celery seed	5	mL
2	tablespoons mustard seed	25	mL
½	teaspoon ground cloves	2	mL
1½	teaspoons turmeric	7	mL

Slice cucumbers as thinly as possible, using food processor, or by hand. Using a large stainless steel, ceramic or glass container, layer cucumbers, onions and pepper strips, sprinkling with salt and a few ice cubes between the layers. Place more ice cubes on top. Cover with a weighted lid; leave for at least 3 hours. (May be left overnight if preparation is done in the evening.) Pour off any liquid; rinse vegetables well under cold water. Drain. In a large preserving kettle, heat vinegar, sugar and spices to the boiling point. Add vegetables to the hot liquid; bring to a boil. Remove from heat. Immediately fill hot sterilized jars with pickles and liquid, sealing with self-sealing lids. Store in a cool dark place.

Makes about 16 jars (each 8 oz/250 mL)

Kumquat and Ginger Marmalade

Make this in January or February when kumquats are in season.

2	pounds fresh kumquats	1	kg
7	cups water	1.75	L
7	cups granulated sugar	1.75	L
1	tablespoon grated fresh ginger (or ½ cup/125 mL preserved ginger, chopped)	15	mL

Slice kumquats thinly. Remove the seeds and place the seeds in a small bowl with 1 cup (250 mL) of the water. Let stand overnight. Combine sliced kumquats in a stainless steel saucepan with remaining 6 cups (1.5 L) water; cover and let stand overnight. The next day, strain the water from the seeds into the kumquat mixture. Keep spooning the liquid from the fruit mixture over the seeds in the strainer, stirring. This will flush the jelly, which has formed, into the kumquat mixture. Discard seeds. Bring kumquat mixture to a boil, reduce heat and simmer for 30 minutes. Add sugar, stirring constantly until it dissolves. Bring to a full boil; boil for about 20 minutes or until mixture sets when tested on a cold saucer. Stir in ginger; let stand for about 5 minutes. Pour into sterilized jars; seal.

Makes about 7 jars (each 8 oz/250 mL)

Treats and Treasures

White Frosted Grapes
A wonderful marriage of flavors.

1	pound small green seedless grapes	500	g
½	pound white chocolate	250	g
1½	teaspoons paraffin wax	7	mL

Wash grapes; dry completely. Cut into small clusters. Place a long skewer or fine knitting needle across the top of a large bowl. This will be used to dry the clusters of chocolate-covered grapes. In a 2-cup (500 mL) measure or small deep bowl, combine white chocolate and paraffin. Soften carefully over hot water. Do not use microwave for this. Remove from heat; stir lightly to complete melting. Dip grape clusters into melted chocolate, shaking off excess coating. Carefully place clusters over skewer to dry. If desired, clusters can also be dried on waxed paper.

Serves 4 to 6

Candied Citrus Peel
Wonderful after dessert with coffee or your favorite chocolates.

10	lemons or limes or grapefruit or oranges or any combination of these fruits	10	
8	cups water	2	L
2½	cups granulated sugar	625	mL

Peel fruits; cut peel into thin julienne strips. Dissolve 1½ cups (375 mL) of the sugar in water; simmer the peel, covered, for approximately 1½ hours. Drain peel in sieve. Place on paper towel to absorb moisture. Preheat oven to 200° F (100° C). Toss peel in a plastic bag with ½ cup (125 mL) sugar to coat. Place on a cookie sheet; bake for 1 hour. Let cool and let air-dry for 20 to 30 minutes. Toss in a plastic bag with remaining sugar. Store in airtight container.

Makes 2 cups (500 mL)

Heavenly Peanut Brittle

A heavenly treat, indeed! A nice gift for a lucky friend.

2	cups granulated sugar	500	mL
1	cup light corn syrup	250	mL
½	cup water	125	mL
1	cup butter	250	mL
1	teaspoon baking soda	5	mL
2	cups roasted peanuts	500	mL

In a large saucepan, combine sugar, corn syrup and water. Heat and stir until sugar dissolves. Blend in butter when syrup boils. Stir often after temperature reaches 280° F (140° C) on a candy thermometer. Continue cooking and stirring to 300° F (150° C) or the hard crack stage. If not using thermometer, this means that the mixture will be very brittle both in the air and if dropped from a spoon into cold water. Cooking time may be 25 to 35 minutes. Remove from heat; stir in baking soda and peanuts, mixing well. Quickly pour onto 2 buttered cookie sheets, spreading evenly. Let cool; break into pieces. Store in a cool place.

Makes about 2 pounds (1 kg)

* Brittle à la Mode
A luscious dessert!

	Heavenly Peanut Brittle		
2	**cups very cold vanilla, coffee or**	500	mL
	chocolate ice cream		
	Liqueur or chocolate sauce (optional)		

Coarsely chop a small amount of peanut brittle (it goes a long way!) with a rolling pin or in a food processor. Place in a small bowl. Make small rounded scoops of ice cream. Roll ice cream in crushed brittle; freeze until ready to use. Serve with your favorite liqueur, chocolate sauce, or as is.

Serves 6 to 8

Chocolate-Coated Almond-Butter Crunch

Delicious crunchy candy. Perfect for gift giving.

1	cup butter	250 mL
1⅓	cups sugar	325 mL
1	tablespoon corn syrup	15 mL
3	tablespoons water	50 mL
1	cup coarsely chopped blanched almonds	250 mL
3	bars (each 4 oz/100 g) milk chocolate	3
1	cup finely chopped unblanched almonds	250 mL

Melt butter in a large saucepan. Add sugar, corn syrup and water. Cook over medium heat, stirring occasionally, until mixture reaches 280° F (140° C) on a candy thermometer. Then stir often until mixture reaches 300° F (150° C) or the hard crack stage (see note below). Quickly mix in the coarsely chopped nuts. Pour onto well-greased cookie sheet; spread on sheet until candy measures approximately 13" x 9" (33 cm x 23 cm). Let cool; turn out onto waxed paper. Melt ½ of the chocolate carefully over hot water; spread over top of the candy. Sprinkle with ½ of the finely chopped nuts; cover with waxed paper and turn over. Melt remaining chocolate; spread on second side. Sprinkle with remaining nuts. Chill; break into pieces. Store in a cool place.

Makes 2 pounds (1 kg)

* If you do not have a candy thermometer, the hard crack stage can be identified by dropping a small amount of syrup into very cold water. It should separate into threads that are hard and brittle. It may take 30 to 35 minutes to reach this stage.

Crazy Candy

No one will guess the ingredients.

2	pounds white chocolate	1	kg
1	can (7 oz/185 g) ruffled Pringles potato chips	1	
1	cup salted peanuts	250	mL

Melt chocolate slowly over simmering water. In a large mixing bowl, by hand, gently crumble potato chips into medium-sized pieces; mix with peanuts. Pour melted chocolate over chips and peanuts; toss to coat well. Drop by small spoonfuls onto foil-lined cookie sheets; refrigerate until firm.

Makes 4 dozen pieces

* For a more sophisticated version, use bittersweet chocolate and pecans or shelled pistachios in the same quantities. Add ¼ cup (50 mL) finely chopped, crystallized ginger.

* Use ½ the recipe with 1 pound (500 g) dark chocolate and ½ the recipe with 1 pound (500 g) white chocolate.

* To dark chocolate, add the zest of 1 orange and 1 teaspoon (5 mL) orange bitters.

Buttered Pecans

¼-½	cup butter	50-125	mL
2	cups (or more) pecan halves	500	mL
	Salt		

Preheat oven to 350° F (180° C). In a heavy skillet over medium heat, melt butter until foamy. Add pecans; stir until well coated. On a large cookie sheet, spread nuts in a single layer. Sprinkle liberally with salt. Bake for 15 to 20 minutes, shaking cookie sheet from time to time. Let nuts cool on paper towels or brown paper. Store in an airtight container. Refrigerate or freeze for long-term storage.

Makes 2 cups (500 mL)

Spiced Pecans

Keep on hand in the freezer for unexpected guests.

3	tablespoons butter	50	mL
1	teaspoon ground cinnamon	5	mL
3-4	tablespoons Worcestershire sauce	50	mL
2-3	garlic cloves, minced	2-3	
	Pinch of cayenne		
1-2	drops hot pepper sauce	1-2	
4	cups pecan halves	1	L

Preheat oven to 300° F (150° C). Melt butter in a fry pan. Add other ingredients; stir. Sauté until nuts are well coated. Place on a cookie sheet in a single layer; toast in oven for 15 minutes, turning nuts after 8 minutes. Remove from oven and spread on paper towel until cool. Store in an airtight container in refrigerator or freezer.

Makes 4 cups (1 L)

Kentucky Bourbon Sauce

Superlative over vanilla ice cream.

½	cup brown sugar	125 mL
½	cup granulated sugar	125 mL
½	cup water	125 mL
½	cup chopped pecans	125 mL
½	cup strawberry jam	125 mL
½	orange with peel, finely chopped	½
½	lemon with peel, finely chopped	½
½	cup bourbon or rye	125 mL

Cook sugars with water until they spin a thread (230° F-234° F/110° C-115° C). Remove from heat; stir in remaining ingredients. Let mixture ripen for 2 to 3 days.

Makes 2 cups (500 mL)

* Serve warm or cold over ice cream.

Grandma Smillie's Mincemeat

Make late in November before the Christmas rush. Grandma Smillie STILL makes this!

4½	pounds medium ground beef	2.25	kg
2¼	pounds ground suet	1	kg
4-5	cans (each 14 oz/398 mL) applesauce	4-5	
4	pounds raisins	2	kg
2	pounds currants	1	kg
2	tablespoons salt	25	mL
1	tablespoon ground cinnamon	15	mL
1	tablespoon ground cloves	15	mL
1	tablespoon ground nutmeg	15	mL
1	tablespoon allspice	15	mL
1½	cups brown sugar	375	mL
2	cups cider vinegar	500	mL
1	cup raspberry vinegar	250	mL
2	jars (each 12 oz/340 g) strawberry or raspberry jam	2	
1	small bottle (2 oz/46 mL) vanilla	1	

In a large skillet, cook ground beef until no longer pink. (Break meat apart as it cooks.) Place in a large crock or pot. Add remaining ingredients; stir. Store in a cool place. May be frozen or refrigerated.

Makes lots and lots!

Index

Index

GOOD FRIENDS COOKBOOK and **FARE FOR FRIENDS**
To order your copies of these cookbooks, cut out and fill in the attached form and send it to P.O. Box 173 Clarkson, Mississauga, Ontario L5J 3Y1.

Canada — Prices include GST (registration no.: R120620489)

Qty.   Amt.

_____ copies of *Good Friends Cookbook* x $18.14   _____

_____ copies of *Fare for Friends* x $16.00   _____

          plus $2.68 postage and handling, per order   _____

                                              Total   _____

Outside Canada — Prices in US funds:

Qty.   Amt.

_____ copies of *Good Friends Cookbook* x $16.95   _____

_____ copies of *Fare for Friends* x $14.95   _____

          plus $2.50 postage and handling, per order   _____

                                              Total   _____

Cheque or money order payable to **Fare for Friends Foundation**, or

Charge to: Visa ☐   Mastercard ☐

Card number _____ Expiry date _____

Name _____

Address _____

_____ City _____

Prov./State _____ Postal/Zip code _____

Signature _____

GOOD FRIENDS COOKBOOK and **FARE FOR FRIENDS**
To order your copies of these cookbooks, cut out and fill in the attached form and send it to P.O. Box 173 Clarkson, Mississauga, Ontario L5J 3Y1.

Canada — Prices include GST (registration no.: R120620489)

Qty.   Amt.

_____ copies of *Good Friends Cookbook* x $18.14   _____

_____ copies of *Fare for Friends* x $16.00   _____

          plus $2.68 postage and handling, per order   _____

                                              Total   _____

Outside Canada — Prices in US funds:

Qty.   Amt.

_____ copies of *Good Friends Cookbook* x $16.95   _____

_____ copies of *Fare for Friends* x $14.95   _____

          plus $2.50 postage and handling, per order   _____

                                              Total   _____

Cheque or money order payable to **Fare for Friends Foundation**, or

Charge to: Visa ☐   Mastercard ☐

Card number _____ Expiry date _____

Name _____

Address _____

_____ City _____

Prov./State _____ Postal/Zip code _____

Signature _____